Healthy Yummies for Young Tummies

Healthy Yummies for Young Tummies

Nutritious Recipes for Children and Their Families

Ann L. Schrader

introduction by Dr. Richard Byyny

RUTLEDGE HILL PRESS
Nashville, Tennessee

This book is dedicated to my Grandma, Ethel Rudd Schrader,
who taught me how to cook with fun; and to my husband,
Rusty, and children, Hilary and Andrew, for all their love
and support.

Copyright © 1993 Ann L. Schrader

Published in Nashville, Tennessee, by Rutledge Hill Press, Inc., 211 Seventh Avenue
North, Nashville, Tennessee 37219

Designed by Julia Pitkin & Stephen Woolverton with large illustrations by Ted Nunes.

Library of Congress Cataloging-in-Publication Data

Schrader, Ann L., 1954-
      Healthy yummies for young tummies / Ann L. Schrader.
          p.   cm.
      Includes index.
      ISBN 1-55853-174-2 : $12.95
      1. Cookery. I. Title.
TX714.S38   1992
641.5—dc20
                                                                                   92-8952
                                                                                   CIP

Printed in the United States of America
   2 3 4 5 6 7 8 — 97 96 95 94

Contents

Preface

Finally, a cookbook for families—adults and children—to use for healthy eating. Good nutrition provides sustenance and improves health and well-being. Unhealthy eating habits adopted in childhood frequently continue into adulthood, resulting in obesity and contributing significantly to half of the most common causes of death in the United States. Excess calories and fat intake are associated with coronary heart disease, strokes, some cancers, diabetes mellitus, and "hardening of the arteries."

Studies indicate that children eat about 20 percent too much fat, consume excess calories, and do not get enough exercise. This results in obese children who, in turn, become obese adults. Obesity not only contributes significantly to diseases, it also results in lack of self-esteem and discrimination. Later in life, the high dietary fat will cause plugs in coronary and other arteries, resulting in heart attacks and premature death. All of this can be prevented, and the best time to start changing and to teach healthy eating to children is now.

The National Cholesterol Education Program recommends, for those over age two, sufficient caloric intake for growth and development without promoting obesity, restriction of fat to less than 30 percent of calories, limiting intake of saturated fats to less than 10 percent of total calories, and limiting cholesterol intake to less than 300 milligrams a day. To accomplish this, we recommend the following: eat more fruits, vegetables, grains, breads, cereals, and beans; eat skim milk products; eat poultry, fish, or small portions of lean red meat; eat few egg yolks; use oils and margarines high in unsaturated fats; choose baked goods made with unsaturated vegetable oils and little egg yolk; and learn to select lower-fat fast foods, especially those which are baked, boiled, or broiled without fat.

Children can learn healthy eating behaviors through experience with healthy meals. Many adults will have to change unhealthy behaviors. Many find the following six steps useful to change unhealthy eating habits: identify eating excess calories and a high-fat diet as a problem; make a commitment to yourself to change to a healthier diet; become aware of your unhealthy eating habits by recording your food intake, your reasons for eating, and your feelings over a two- to three-day period and see what you can change; implement an action plan

Preface

based upon gradually changing high-fat foods for carbohydrates and decreasing total calories if you are fat; evaluate your results and reward yourself without using food; and, finally, develop a plan to sustain the changes.

As part of the action plan, I frequently recommend starting with one meal, for instance, breakfast. Establish a goal to eat low-fat meals with appropriate calories for three of seven days each week. After accomplishing this, you can extend it to five days and eventually to seven. Then repeat the process with dinner and, finally, lunch.

It may be helpful to know that you can change your palate or taste preferences over time as you eat food with less fat. You will eventually find that a high fat-meal tastes unusual to you. Some people find that a "splurge" meal one day per week, when they can eat a less healthy meal, is helpful in sticking with the changes on other days. Most people find that they don't "splurge" very much on these less restricted days, and overall their eating is greatly improved.

Remember that motivation to change and to sustain a change will be enhanced by having role models and supporters. When the entire family changes, each member can provide the others the support they need.

Ann Schrader has done her homework and appropriate research with recipes. Her book, *Healthy Yummies for Young Tummies,* provides useful and tasty recipes to use in healthy family eating.

What better gift can you give your family and children than healthy eating habits that will maintain health and well-being, prevent disease and disability, and avoid the burden of obesity.

Richard L. Byyny, M.D.
Professor of Medicine
Head, Division of Internal Medicine
University of Colorado
School of Medicine

Introduction

The reader might ask why I decided to write this cookbook. As a mother of young children, I was interested in their health. The belief that "You are what you eat" had been ingrained in my beliefs, and I was concerned for their nutritional well-being, as well as my own.

Prior to having children, my husband and I focused on a healthy lifestyle. We exercised regularly and prepared foods that were low in sodium, cholesterol, sugar. and fat. We felt good, and we enjoyed our meals. When our children were born, we assumed they would eat what we prepared for them. We liked it; so they would like it. We were in for a rude awakening!

As my children began eating table food, I noticed their dislike for most foods I considered healthy. Frustrated, I searched the bookstores and library but found no cookbooks that were aimed at healthy eating for young children and their parents. As I refused to consider cooking two meals at a time, I decided to try to compile a group of recipes that were healthy and would appeal to my entire family.

We had a delightful time experimenting with new recipes. Each member of the family was included, and we talked about the foods we liked eating and those we didn't like. I took a lot of notes and observed everyone's reactions as we tried new recipes and modified old ones.

After each meal, we talked about what we had eaten, then voted—thumbs up or thumbs down—on each recipe's fate. At the beginning there were a lot of thumbs down, but we were having fun and were working as a team. At times it was very difficult to combine healthy food and tastiness into into a successful dish, but we kept trying.

Not only was I concerned with my family's opinions, I wanted to know what the experts in nutrition and medicine had to say. So while my children attended story time, I searched the library for pertinent material. As I researched healthy family eating, I concluded that the accepted standards for good nutrition came from the American Heart and Cancer associations. Hence, the goal of this cookbook became to develop a collection of recipes that met the American Heart and Cancer associations' dietary guidelines for healthy family eating. The other prerequisite for a recipe to gain entry into this book was that it had to meet the high approval standards of my tasters: my

Introduction

children, Hilary and Andrew; my husband, Rusty; other young children I knew between the ages of three and twelve years; and, yes, myself.

This was not an easy task, as parents can well imagine. While trying at least one new recipe a day for more than two years, I experienced lots of rejections! The result is *Healthy Yummies for Young Tummies*, a cookbook I use every day. Mealtimes are so different in our house now. Hilary and Andrew look forward to them because they enjoy the food, and we argue less about what we are having for dinner. Much less food goes down the garbage disposal, and I seldom have apprehension about whether my efforts will be enjoyed. I am confident that I am preparing nutritional meals and a pleasant environment for my family.

I hope you will benefit from my efforts. By using *Healthy Yummies for Young Tummies*, you should be able to plan and prepare menus that are healthy and enjoyable for the whole family. This cookbook will give you the positive approach to combining nutrition with "good tasting food." You will feel better knowing that you are taking charge of your family's eating habits and living a healthier lifestyle. I have done the research, tested the recipes, provided nutritional analysis, and even planned menus for you.

Healthy Yummies for Young Tummies is user friendly. The layout makes it easy to read, and the recipes are easy to follow. Also included are valuable nutritional tips

and cartoon illustrations to give your whole family a good laugh!

The guidelines I followed in developing my recipes were aimed at results that would be low in cholesterol, sugar, sodium, and fat. Specifically, during one day I prepare meals that provide a total food intake of 55 to 60 percent carbohydrates, 15 percent proteins, and 25 to 30 percent fats. In addition, I limit sodium usage to less than 3,300 milligrams and cholesterol to less than 300 milligrams per day.

American Cancer Association research indicates reduction of fat, sodium, caffeine, cholesterol, and alcohol reduces the risk of cancer. Their findings also point to the use of beta-carotene and fiber as aids in the prevention of cancer. The American Heart Association believes that reducing cholesterol and fat reduces the risk of heart disease, the leading cause of death in our country.

At this writing, the most up-to-date research on fat and cholesterol pertaining to this book is compiled in the "Report of the Expert Panel on Blood Cholesterol Levels in Children and Adolescents." This report is under the auspices of the National Cholesterol Education Program and was published September 1991.

Their recommended "pattern of nutrient intake" for healthy children and adolescents is: saturated fat to be less than 10 percent of total calories; total fat average to be no more than 30 percent of total calories; dietary cholesterol to be no more than 300 mg per day. The nutritional analysis at the side of each recipe should help in providing meals that stay within the recommended guidelines

The report reminds the reader that part of the goal is for "sufficient calories for growth and development" to be provided and consumed. (Be aware that when reducing total fat calories, children may not get enough calories and may substitute empty sugar/junk food calories that will not fulfill their nutritional requirements.) In addition, the report states that the major contributor of saturated fatty acids in children's diets is dairy products. By choosing low-fat dairy products, i.e., low- or nonfat milk, low-fat cheeses, and low- or non-fat yogurts, the saturated fat in children's diets can be lowered while maintaining other necessary nutrients.

In my research, I explored specific dietary needs of children. I was surprised to find that only a limited amount of information on this subject is available to the average parent. I was able to conclude that after the age of two years, children's needs appear to be about the same as adults, the major difference being caloric requirements. Roughly, between the ages of four to six, children need up to 1,700 calories; between seven and ten, they need 2,400 calories. Adult males require 2,700 calories and adult females 2,000. Again, the nutritional analysis should help you provide meals that respect these recommendations

This introduction is not intended as a complete review of information available on healthy eating. It is just a summary of enough facts to remind the reader of my purpose and of where this cookbook is headed. I have purposely tried to keep it short. As a working mother, I have found that a lengthy introduction in a cookbook is a barrier to its use. I am lucky if I can find the time to prepare a meal! If you are interested in more information, I refer you to the bibliography at the end of the book.

For your ease in beginning a new cooking style, I have included a list of staples and utensil requirements that are helpful for healthy cooking. You will find these at the beginning of the cookbook. Please review them first before beginning your meal planning. I found that when I changed my focus to healthy eating, my cupboard was lacking in many ingredients. It took me a while to stock my pantry; indeed, it took me awhile to find some of the ingredients at the food store, although the situation is much improved today. My suggestion for getting started would be to buy a large non-stick pan; it's a must. Buy ingredients as you need them in a recipe.

At the back of the cookbook, you will find six weeks of preplanned menus. I find menu planning time consuming, so please avail yourself of my efforts. I did it for you!

When you prepare your own menus, I would offer some general suggestions. On the top of my list would be: Eat a wide variety of foods, and nothing in excess.

Introduction

Other ideas are:

1. When using oils, select corn, safflower, olive, soybean, or canola.
2. Eat only two to three eggs a week.
3. Eat twenty to thirty grams of fiber a day. This includes whole grain breads, bran cereals, vegetables, cooked dried peas and beans, and fruits.
4. Eat foods high in vitamins A and C (beta-carotene). This would include yellow-orange vegetables and fruits, such as carrots, winter squash, sweet potatoes, peaches, oranges, lemons, grapefruit, berries, and cantaloupe; dark green leafy vegetables, such as spinach, watercress, broccoli, asparagus, and tomatoes; the cabbage family, such as cabbage, cauliflower, turnips, radishes, and brussels sprouts.

To assist you in planning your dietary intake, I have nutritionally analyzed the recipes. The analysis is provided at the side of each recipe. I employed a software program designed by nutritionists to analyze the nutritional value of each ingredient. When developing their program, these nutritionists relied on U.S. Department of Agriculture standards for food values and interpretations compiled by the Case Western Reserve Medical School.

All of the foods mentioned above are items I add to every meal, fresh or steamed, that my children especially love, and no recipe is needed. Also, our favorite meal, which we have weekly, is grilled fish, baked potatoes, and steamed broccoli. Probably the easiest, it is also our most healthy meal. Please include it in your menu.

Obviously, I cannot guarantee that everyone will enjoy each of these recipes. I often find that my own children's likes and dislikes change as the wind blows. In my reading, I found a study that showed that the younger a child is, the more willing he is to try a new food. By the time a child is four years old, he will be ready to try a new food only 7 percent of the time. Therefore, if eating by healthy dietary guidelines will be a big change in your family's eating habits, I would suggest that you try a few new things at a time. Even if a recipe does not receive rave reviews the first time you try it, you should reintroduce it several times before you give up. Other than food, children love atmosphere: funny food names, candles, crazy and frequently changed placemats, different textures, lukewarm temperatures, and brightly colored foods. Allowing your children to help in preparing the foods they eat also adds to the success of the meal. Calm classical music seems to help, too. At least it helps the chief chef!

Happy, healthy eating!

Necessary Staples for Your Pantry

Baking Ingredients

Almond flavoring
Baking soda
Brown sugar
Coconut flavoring
Cornstarch
Dark molasses

Dark raisins
Featherweight low-sodium baking powder
Granulated sugar
Honey
Nonfat powdered milk
Pure vanilla extract

Canned Goods

Hunt's no-salt-added tomato paste
Kraft Parmesan Cheese
Hunt's no-salt-added tomato sauce
Hunt's no-salt-added whole tomatoes

Mayonnaise
Pritikin chicken broth
Sliced black olives
Kraft Miracle Whip Fat-Free Imitation

Dairy and Condiments

Apple juice concentrate
Dry white wine (no salt)
Kraft Philadelphia Free Cream Cheese
Kraft Reduced Fat Mild Cheddar Cheese
Lemons
Nonfat milk

Nonfat yogurt (Dannon)
Red wine
Salt-free club soda
SherryWhite vinegar
Vermouth

Oils

Canola oil
Corn oil
Olive oil
PAM baking spray

Promise margarine
Safflower oil
Sesame oil

Necessary Staples

Grains

All-purpose flour
Barley
Bulgur wheat
Cornmeal
Couscous
Long-grain brown rice
Long-grain white rice

Oat bran
Quaker Old-Fashioned Oats
Quick Malt-o-Meal
Soy flour
Stone-ground whole-wheat flour
Wheat bran
Wheat germ

Spices and Seasonings

Bay leaves
Black pepper
Cayenne pepper
Chili powder
Chives
Cinnamon
Cream of Tartar
Crushed red pepper flakes
Curry powder
Dried basil leaves
Dried cilantro
Dried dill
Dried oregano leaves
Dried sage
Dry mustard
Garlic powder
Ground cloves

Ground cumin
Ground ginger
Italian herb seasoning
Low-sodium soy sauce
Mace
Marjoram
Minced garlic cloves
Mrs. Dash
Nutmeg
Poppy seeds
Pumpkin pie spice
Rosemary
Saffron*
Salt substitute
Sesame seeds
Tarragon
Thyme leaves

*Very expensive, only buy when ready to use.

Cooking Utensils and Miscellaneous

Non-stick 8" and/or 12" frying pan
Non-stick wok
Non-stick griddle

Saucepan with tight-fitting lid
Non-stick muffin pan
Toothpicks

Breakfasts and Beverages

Brown Sugar Oatmeal

1⅛ cups Quaker Old-Fashioned Oats
3 cups water
1 tablespoon brown sugar
1 tablespoon dark raisins
1 teaspoon cinnamon
½ cup skim milk

Per serving:

135 calories
12% of calories from fat
5.5 gm protein
24.7 gm carbohydrates
0.8 tsp sugar
1.8 gm fat
19.2 mg sodium
0.5 mg cholesterol

In a medium saucepan bring the water to a boil. Stir in the oatmeal and reduce the heat to medium low. Cook for 5 minutes, stirring occasionally, until the water is absorbed. Remove the pan from the heat. Add the brown sugar, raisins, and cinnamon, stirring until blended. Cover and let rest for 5 minutes.

Pour the oatmeal mixture into 4 bowls. Stir in a little milk and serve. A favorite on cold, snowy days and early summer mornings.

Serves 4.

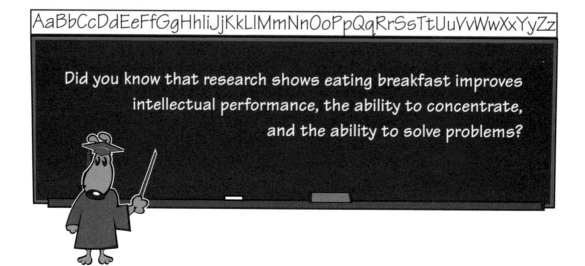

AaBbCcDdEeFfGgHhIiJjKkLlMmNnOoPpQqRrSsTtUuVvWwXxYyZz

Did you know that research shows eating breakfast improves intellectual performance, the ability to concentrate, and the ability to solve problems?

Swirly Oatmeal

1⅓ cups Quaker Old-Fashioned Oats
3 cups water
2 teaspoons low sugar fruit preserves
  (we like grape, strawberry, or raspberry)
½ cup skim milk (optional)

In a medium saucepan bring the water to a boil. Add the oatmeal and reduce the heat to medium low. Cook, stirring occasionally, for 5 minutes or until the water is absorbed. Remove from the heat, cover, and let rest for 5 minutes.

Pour the oatmeal into 4 bowls. Gently swirl ½ teaspoon of the preserves into the oatmeal. Serve immediately. (You can add milk after the child enjoys the swirled effect, but it will ruin the swirl.)

Serves 4.

Per serving:

121 calories
13% of calories from fat
5.4 gm protein
20.9 gm carbohydrates
0.3 tsp sugar
1.8 gm fat
16.9 mg sodium
0.5 cholesterol

Saturday morning choices

Studies suggest that up to 70% of commercials on Saturday morning children's television are for food products. Of those, up to 80% are considered low in nutritional value.

Saturday morning time might be spent by having one of the breakfasts, and then taking off for a family activity such as swimming, aerobics, skiing, ice skating, or hiking.

Hominy and Cheese

3 cups water
¾ cup Quaker Quick Grits
½ cup grated Kraft Mild Reduced Fat
   Cheddar Cheese
½ cup skim milk

In a medium saucepan bring the water to a boil.
Reduce the heat to medium low and add the grits. Cook
for 4 to 5 minutes, stirring occasionally, until the water is
absorbed. While the hominy is cooking, grate cheese.

   When the grits are done, remove from the heat and stir
in the cheese. Cover the pan and allow to rest for 5 minutes.

   Divide the grits among four bowls. Stir a little milk into each, then serve.
   Serves 4.

Per serving:
160 calories
16% of calories from fat
7.6 gm protein
25.6 gm carbohydrates
0 tsp sugar
2.9 gm fat
497.3 mg sodium
10.5 mg cholesterol

Mapley Malt-o-Meal

3¼ cups water
⅔ cup Quick Malt-o-Meal
2 tablespoons Aunt Jemima Lite Syrup (or real
   maple syrup)
½ cup skim milk

In a medium saucepan bring the water to a boil. Add
the Malt-o-Meal and reduce the heat to medium low.
Cook for 1 to 2 minutes, stirring frequently, until the
water is absorbed.

   Remove from the heat. Stir in the maple syrup, cover,
and let rest 5 minutes.

   Pour the Malt-o-Meal into 4 bowls, stir in a little milk, and serve.

   Variation: We also enjoy Malt-o-Meal with cinnamon, brown sugar, and raisins.
For amounts, refer to Brown Sugar Oatmeal on page 2.
   Serves 4.

Per serving:
55 calories
1% of calories from fat
1.6 gm protein
12.0 gm carbohydrates
1.6 tsp sugar
0.1 gm fat
143.9 mg sodium
0.5 mg cholesterol

Oatmeal Pancakes

½ cup Quaker Old-Fashioned Oats
¼ cup whole-wheat flour
¼ cup all-purpose flour
2 teaspoons low-sodium baking powder (Featherweight)
½ teaspoon baking soda
¾ cup buttermilk
¼ cup skim milk
1 tablespoon frozen apple juice concentrate
1 tablespoon corn oil
2 egg whites
¼ cup maple syrup
PAM baking spray

Per pancake:

88 calories
19% of calories from fat
3.0 gm protein
14.9 gm carbohydrates
1.3 tsp sugar
1.9 gm fat
89 mg sodium
0.8 mg cholesterol

Heat a nonstick skillet or griddle to medium high heat.

In a large bowl combine the dry ingredients. Set aside. In a medium bowl combine the liquid ingredients with a wire whisk. Stir the liquid into the dry ingredients with a spoon.

Spray a griddle with baking spray. Using a large serving spoon, pour the pancake batter onto the griddle. Cook the pancakes on each side until golden brown, usually about 1 minute on each side.

Serve with a little Promise margarine and maple syrup.

Makes 10 pancakes.

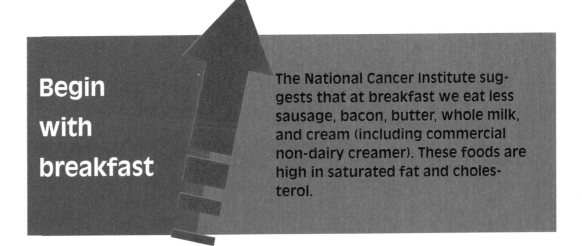

Begin
with
breakfast

The National Cancer Institute suggests that at breakfast we eat less sausage, bacon, butter, whole milk, and cream (including commercial non-dairy creamer). These foods are high in saturated fat and cholesterol.

Breakfast Cookies

This recipe was found in the February 1989 issue of *Good Housekeeping* magazine. I modified it to meet our dietary interests.

½ cup **Promise margarine, softened**
1 cup **firmly packed brown sugar**
1½ cups **stone-ground whole-wheat flour**
1½ cups **unsweetened applesauce**
1 cup **Quaker Old-Fashioned Oats**
⅔ cup **oat bran**
½ cup **nonfat powdered milk**
2 **egg whites**
1 teaspoon **baking soda**
1 teaspoon **cinnamon**
1 teaspoon **low-sodium baking powder (Featherweight)**
½ teaspoon **ground cloves**
1 cup **dark raisins**
½ cup **chopped walnuts**
1 8-ounce package **Kraft Philadelphia Free Cream Cheese, softened**

Per serving:

248 calories
31% of calories from fat
6.7 gm protein
38.8 gm carbohydrates
3.4 tsp sugar
8.6 gm fat
247.2 mg sodium
2.9 mg cholesterol

In a large bowl cream the margarine and brown sugar with an electric beater. Add the next 10 ingredients, beating until well combined. Stir in the raisins and walnuts.

Drop the cookie batter by the tablespoonful onto a nonstick cookie sheet, 2 to 3 inches apart. Bake in a 375° oven for 10 to 12 minutes, or until set. Remove from the cookie sheet immediately and cool on a wire rack.

When cooled, spread half the cookies with 2 teaspoons of softened cream cheese. Top each with another cookie. Place each cookie in a plastic sandwich bag, or individually wrap in plastic wrap. Freeze.

Thaw cookies as needed in the refrigerator overnight before serving. A great on-the-go breakfast for the school bus, or at the reservoir as you watch the sunrise.

Makes 16 big cookies.

Granola

4 cups Quaker Old-Fashioned Oats
1 cup unsweetened wheat flake cereal
¼ cup sunflower seeds
¼ cup raw, unsalted peanuts
⅛ cup sesame seeds
¼ cup unsweetened flaked coconut
½ cup nonfat powdered milk
½ cup raisins
¼ cup corn oil
1 teaspoon cinnamon
¼ teaspoon nutmeg
½ cup orange juice
4 tablespoons frozen apple juice concentrate
1 teaspoon vanilla extract
½ cup chopped dates (8)

Per serving:

196 calories
27% of calories from fat
7.6 gm protein
29.4 gm carbohydrates
0.2 tsp sugar
6 gm fat
45.0 mg sodium
0.5 mg cholesterol

In a large roasting pan combine the first 11 ingredients. Stir until completely blended.

In a small bowl combine the orange juice, apple juice, and vanilla. Pour ⅓ of the mixture over the dry ingredients and mix well.

Place the roasting pan in a 275° oven for 15 minutes. Remove the pan and add another ⅓ of the liquid. Stir well. Return to the oven and bake for another 15 minutes. Add the remaining liquid to the granola and stir well. Bake in the oven for another 15 minutes. Stir in the chopped dates.

Store the granola in an airtight container in the refrigerator. Serve granola with milk as a cereal, with fresh fruit and yogurt as a light meal, or alone as a quick snack.

Makes 12 half-cup servings.

The news is good

Fortunately, lots of foods kids like are good for them. Most breakfast cereals are low in fat (but watch for sodium and sugar content), as well as pasta, lean meats, bread, tuna packed in water, skinless chicken, and fruit.

French Toast

PAM baking spray
3 egg whites
⅓ cup skim milk
¼ teaspoon vanilla extract
¼ teaspoon cinnamon
4 to 6 slices of bread (preferably
**   stone-ground whole-wheat)**
Powdered sugar (optional)
¼ cup maple syrup

Per serving:

114 calories
5% of calories from fat
5.6 gm protein
22.1 gm carbohydrates
2.5 tsp sugar
0.7 gm fat
169.0 mg sodium
1.3 mg cholesterol

Spray a nonstick griddle with baking spray. Heat it to medium high.

In a medium bowl combine the egg whites, milk, vanilla extract, and cinnamon, and mix well with a wire whisk. Pour the mixture into a pie pan.

Soak the bread in the egg mixture. Cook the toast on the heated griddle until slightly brown on each side, usually 1 to 2 minutes on each side.

Sprinkle with a pinch of powdered sugar and top with maple syrup.

Time-saving hint: Double or triple this recipe. Place the French Toast you do not use in plastic bags, 2 slices per bag, and freeze. Reheat in the toaster when ready to eat.

Serves 4.

BON JOUR!

Bubble Trouble

Ice
3 ounces sodium-free club soda
4 ounces fruit juice (we like pineapple, cherry, apple, or cranberry)

Place the ice in a glass. Add the club soda and then the fruit juice. Watch for bubbles!
  Serves 1.

Per serving:

74 calories
1% of calories from fat
0.1 gm protein
18.8 gm carbohydrates
1.3 tsp sugar
0.1 gm fat
20.6 mg sodium
0 mg cholesterol

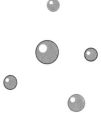

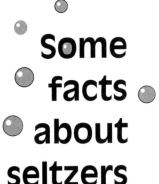

Some facts about seltzers

If you're buying seltzer and sodas to cut down on calories and sodium, read the labels carefully. The Food and Drug Administration defines seltzer as filtered carbonated tap water and club soda as filtered carbonated tap water with minerals and mineral salts containing sodium. Seltzer with fruit flavors added are still a sodium-free noncaloric drink, but are called soda. Watch for sodas that contain sodium but falsely use the term "seltzer." Also, just because the label says "no sucrose" doesn't mean other sweeteners haven't been used.

Grapenade

1 6-ounce can grape juice concentrate
1 6-ounce can lemonade concentrate
¼ cup fresh lemon juice (½ lemon)
6 cups water

In a 2-quart pitcher combine all of the ingredients.
Serve over ice, with straws of course.
   Makes 8 8-ounce servings.

Per serving:

125 calories
1% of calories from fat
0.8 gm protein
31.5 gm carbohydrates
3 tsp sugar
0.1 gm fat
5.3 mg sodium
0 mg cholesterol

Spiced Apple Cider

A Halloween tradition that we serve in our home while carving the pumpkins, this
recipe makes the house smell wonderful!

1 quart unsweetened apple cider
½ cup orange juice
1 stick cinnamon
4 whole cloves
¼ teaspoon ground allspice

Per serving:

66 calories
2% of calories from fat
0.2 gm protein
16.2 gm carbohydrates
0 tsp sugar
0.2 gm fat
3.7 mg sodium
0 mg cholesterol

In a large saucepan combine all of the ingredients.
Heat to boiling, then reduce the heat to low. Cover and
simmer for 20 minutes. Strain and serve.
   Serves 8.

Pineapple Cooler

A wonderful summertime drink. Serve topped with a fresh pineapple slice and cherry, à la straw.

½ **cup frozen pineapple-orange juice concentrate,
   slightly thawed**
½ **ripe banana**
1 **cup water**
⅓ **cup nonfat powdered milk**
½ **teaspoon coconut flavoring**
6 **ice cubes**

Per serving:
51 calories
2% of calories from fat
2.2 gm protein
10.6 gm carbohydrates
0 tsp sugar
0.1 gm fat
31.3 mg sodium
1 mg cholesterol

In a blender combine all of the ingredients except the ice cubes. Process until smooth, approximately 20 seconds. With the blender running, add the ice cubes, 1 at a time. Process until the ice cubes are fully chopped.
   Serves 4.

AaBbCcDdEeFfGgHhIiJjKkLlMmNnOoPpQqRrSsTtUuVvWwXxYyZz

If your child won't drink milk, try yogurt, low-fat cheese and cottage cheese, or flavored milk. Try to serve low-fat varieties of dairy products rather than eliminate them. They're rich in protein, calcium, and vitamins A and D.

Strawberry-Banana Shake

1 pint plain nonfat yogurt
6 frozen strawberries
½ ripe banana
½ cup orange juice
1 tablespoon wheat germ (optional)
1 tablespoon honey
4 to 6 ice cubes

Per serving:

85 calories
4% of calories from fat
3.6 gm protein
18.2 gm carbohydrates
0 tsp sugar
0.4 gm fat
40.6 mg sodium
0.1 mg cholesterol

In a blender combine all of the ingredients. Blend until fairly smooth and frothy.

Variation: Instead of strawberries and banana, you may double their amounts and have only one flavor. For a peach shake, use one cup of fresh peaches, peeled and sliced.

Makes 4 small shakes.

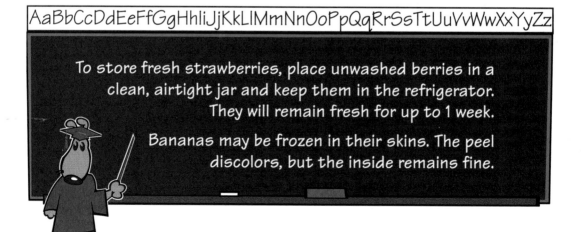

AaBbCcDdEeFfGgHhIiJjKkLlMmNnOoPpQqRrSsTtUuVvWwXxYyZz

To store fresh strawberries, place unwashed berries in a clean, airtight jar and keep them in the refrigerator. They will remain fresh for up to 1 week.

Bananas may be frozen in their skins. The peel discolors, but the inside remains fine.

Soups and
Salads

Beet Red Soup

3 tablespoons white wine
½ cup chopped white onion
1 small leek, washed and thinly sliced
3 medium red potatoes, peeled and thinly sliced
1 6-ounce beet, peeled and thinly sliced
1 13¾-ounce can Pritikin chicken broth
2 teaspoons lemon juice
1 cup plain nonfat yogurt
½ cup skim milk
Pepper to taste

Per serving:

93 calories
3% of calories from fat
5.4 gm protein
16.3 gm carbohydrates
0 tsp sugar
0.3 gm fat
102.8 mg sodium
1.2 mg cholesterol

In a medium saucepan heat the wine and sauté the onion and leek for 10 minutes, or until the onion is soft and clear.

Add the potatoes, beet, broth, and lemon juice, and bring to a boil. Cover and simmer for 40 minutes, stirring occasionally, or until the potatoes and beets are tender. Cool for 5 to 10 minutes.

Pour the cooled mixture into a blender and process until smooth. Return to the saucepan and add the yogurt and milk. Simmer over low heat until warm all the way through. Season with pepper to taste.

Serves 6.

Kids and play !

All the hype about kids learning computer skills and better hand-eye coordination from video games is just that—hype. Encourage children to play outdoors whenever weather permits. It will strengthen social, decision-making, and problem-solving skills, all of which are important aspects of intelligence and independence.

Carrot and Tomato Soup

A beautiful orange soup!

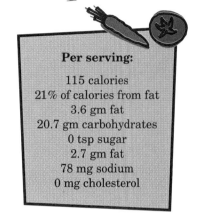

1 tablespoon corn oil
½ yellow onion, chopped
½ pound carrots, peeled and sliced (about 4 carrots)
¼ teaspoon curry powder
6 large, ripe plum tomatoes
1 13¾-ounce can Pritikin chicken broth
1 cup water
½ teaspoon basil
Pepper to taste
1 cup cooked rice (optional)

Per serving:

115 calories
21% of calories from fat
3.6 gm fat
20.7 gm carbohydrates
0 tsp sugar
2.7 gm fat
78 mg sodium
0 mg cholesterol

In a large saucepan sauté the onions in the corn oil over medium high heat for 5 minutes. Add the carrots and curry, stirring well. Cover and cook over low heat for 20 minutes, stirring occasionally.

In a separate saucepan filled with boiling water, submerge the tomatoes and boil them for 1 minute. Remove with a fork, peel off the skin, and slice. Add the sliced tomatoes to the carrot mixture, along with the chicken broth and water. Bring the mixture to a boil. Cover and simmer for 20 minutes. Add the basil and pepper to taste.

Transfer approximately ¾ of the vegetables into a blender. Process until smooth and return to the soup mixture. Add the cooked rice, if desired. Stir to blend. Serve hot.

Serves 6.

Curried Tomato Noodle Soup

1 tablespoon olive oil
1 onion, chopped
1 clove garlic, minced
1½ teaspoons curry powder
2 14-ounce cans no-salt-added whole tomatoes
¼ teaspoon cinnamon
2 13¾-ounce cans Pritikin chicken broth
10 ounces angel hair pasta, cooked

> **Per serving:**
>
> 134 calories
> 15% of calories from fat
> 5.1 gm protein
> 24.3 gm carbohydrates
> 0 tsp sugar
> 2.2 gm fat
> 74.2 mg sodium
> 0 mg cholesterol

In a heavy soup pot heat the oil over medium heat. Add the onion and sauté for 5 minutes, stirring frequently. Add the garlic and curry powder, and cook over low heat for 5 minutes.

Drain the tomato liquid into the soup pot. Chop the tomatoes and add them to the soup mixture. Add the cinnamon and 1 can of the chicken broth to the pot. Cover and simmer over low heat for 20 minutes.

With a slotted spoon transfer the solid ingredients from the soup pot into a blender. Purée and return the mixture to the pot. Add the other can of broth and heat through.

Divide the pasta among 8 bowls. Ladle the soup over the pasta. Combine any remaining pasta and soup and store in the refrigerator. This heats up well as leftovers!

Serves 8.

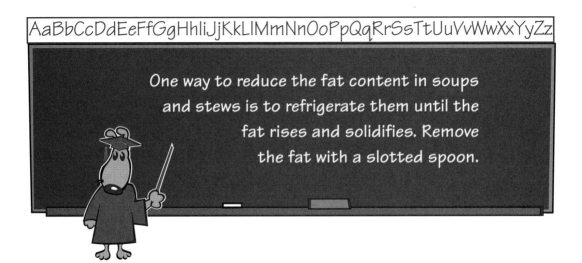

AaBbCcDdEeFfGgHhIiJjKkLlMmNnOoPpQqRrSsTtUuVvWwXxYyZz

One way to reduce the fat content in soups and stews is to refrigerate them until the fat rises and solidifies. Remove the fat with a slotted spoon.

East Indian Chicken Soup

PAM baking spray
1 teaspoon olive oil
½ cup diced onion
1 carrot, sliced
1 stalk celery with leaves, sliced
½ Red Delicious apple, diced
½ cup diced green pepper
1 cup diced raw chicken breast
⅛ cup all-purpose flour
½ teaspoon curry powder
2 13¾-ounce cans Pritikin chicken broth
¼ teaspoon nutmeg
½ teaspoon cloves
1 16-ounce can no-salt-added tomatoes
1 tablespoon dried parsley
2 cups cooked rice
½ cup raisins
Pepper to taste

Per serving:

199 calories
10% of calories from fat
11 gm protein
36.3 gm carbohydrates
0 tsp sugar
2.3 gm fat
139.5 mg sodium
14.7 mg cholesterol

Spray a large soup pan lightly with baking spray. In the prepared pan heat the olive oil over medium heat. Add the onion, carrot, celery, apple, green pepper, and chicken pieces. Stir frequently until the chicken is cooked, approximately 8 to 10 minutes.

Sprinkle the flour and curry powder over the mixture and stir over low heat for 2 minutes. Slowly stir in the chicken broth, then add the nutmeg, cloves, tomatoes and their juice, and the parsley. Cover and simmer for 1 hour, stirring occasionally.

Add the rice and raisins, cooking until the rice is heated through, another 5 to 10 minutes. Season with pepper to taste.

Great with corn bread for a complete dinner meal.

Serves 6.

Siamese (If You Please) Lentil Soup

1 cup rinsed lentils
3 cups Pritikin chicken broth
2 stalks celery, chopped
½ medium onion, finely chopped
¾ teaspoon curry powder
Dash garlic powder

In a medium saucepan combine the lentils, broth, celery, and onion. Bring the broth to a boil. Reduce the heat, cover, and simmer for 30 to 40 minutes, or until the lentils are soft. Add the seasonings and serve.
   Serves 6.

Per serving:

60 calories
7% of calories from fat
4.4 gm protein
10.4 gm carbohydrates
0 tsp sugar
0.5 gm fat
96.8 mg sodium
0 mg cholesterol

Fruit Soup

1 cup applesauce (no sugar added)
2 egg whites
1 tablespoon honey
1 tablespoon grated lemon rind
Cinnamon

In a blender combine the first 4 ingredients. Blend. Divide the applesauce mixture among 4 bowls. Top with cinnamon. It is easy, quick, and good.
   Serves 4.

Per serving:

50 calories
0% of calories from fat
1.8 gm protein
11.4 gm carbohydrates
0 tsp sugar
0 gm fat
26.3 mg sodium
0 mg cholesterol

Hearty Friendship Soup

This recipe is a combination of recipes given to me by my sister-in-law, Patti Felton, and my children's babysitter, Sharon Gatlin. They buy lots of varieties of beans, combine them in an attractive bag, and give them as gifts with the recipe included.

A great gift idea for school organizations and scout troops!

We enjoy the soup with corn bread or over rice.

1 16-ounce package 15-bean soup, seasoning packet discarded
2 quarts water
1 ham hock, all visible fat removed
¼ teaspoon pepper
1 large onion, chopped
4 stalks celery, sliced
2 carrots, sliced
2 14½-ounce cans no-salt-added stewed tomatoes
1 clove garlic, minced

Per serving:

187 calories
7% of calories from fat
14 gm protein
30 gm carbohydrates
0 tsp sugar
1.5 gm fat
218.1 mg sodium
8 mg cholesterol

Begin the night before by rinsing the beans in water. Place the beans in a large plastic or glass bowl and cover with water. Set aside to soak overnight.

Drain the beans and place in a large, heavy soup pot. Cover with 2 quarts of water. Trim the fat from the ham hock and place in the soup pot. Bring the water to a boil over medium high heat. Reduce the heat to low and cover. Simmer for 1 hour and 30 minutes to 2 hours, stirring occasionally. Skim the fat from the broth with a piece of lettuce or a slotted spoon.

Add the remaining ingredients and simmer for an additional 30 minutes or until the carrots are soft, stirring occasionally.

Remove the ham hock. Cut the meat from the ham hock into bite-sized pieces and return to the soup.

Serves 12.

Minestrone

Great with sourdough bread and grapefruit.

1 tablespoon olive oil
1 large carrot, thinly sliced
1 large stalk celery, diced
1 potato, diced
1 onion, diced
¼ pound frozen Italian-cut green beans
½ cup coarsely shredded green cabbage
2 13¾-ounce cans Pritikin chicken broth
1 14½-ounce can no-salt-added tomatoes
1 teaspoon oregano
1 zucchini, thinly sliced
½ cup uncooked macaroni
1 8-ounce can no-salt-added red kidney beans, drained and rinsed
1 8-ounce can no-salt-added butter (lima) beans, drained and
   rinsed
1 8-ounce can no-salt-added tomato sauce
5 ounces (½ package) frozen spinach
Parmesan cheese

Per serving:

140 calories
16% of calories from fat
7.8 gm protein
23.8 gm carbohydrates
0 tsp sugar
2.5 gm fat
126.8 mg sodium
0 mg cholesterol

In a nonstick skillet heat the oil over medium high heat. Sauté the first 5 vegetables in the oil until they are lightly browned, about 5 to 7 minutes.

Transfer the vegetables to a large soup pot. Add the cabbage, broth, tomatoes, and oregano, and bring to a boil. Cover, reduce the heat, and simmer for 15 minutes. Add zucchini and macaroni and simmer for an additional 20 minutes, stirring occasionally.

Add the kidney and butter beans, tomato sauce, and spinach, cooking until heated through. Serve in soup bowls. Let the children add their own Parmesan cheese.

Serves 8.

Meanie Greenie Zucchini Soup

A Saint Paddy's Day delight!

1 cup Pritikin chicken broth
1 pound zucchini, sliced
⅛ teaspoon basil
⅛ teaspoon thyme
½ teaspoon marjoram
2 cups skim milk
Dash paprika

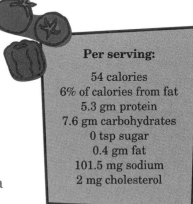

Per serving:

54 calories
6% of calories from fat
5.3 gm protein
7.6 gm carbohydrates
0 tsp sugar
0.4 gm fat
101.5 mg sodium
2 mg cholesterol

In a medium soup pot, bring the chicken broth to a boil. Add the zucchini, cover, and simmer for 5 to 7 minutes. Cool. Add the spices. Purée the mixture in a blender. Return the mixture to the pot, add the milk, and heat over medium heat. Top with a dash of paprika.
   Serves 4.

AaBbCcDdEeFfGgHhIiJjKkLlMmNnOoPpQqRrSsTtUuVvWwXxYyZz

Tips for soups: Always start with cold water. This allows the flavor from the meat bones to flow into the broth.

Whenever possible, cool the soup before putting it into the refrigerator. This saves your refrigerator motor extra work.

Hearty Mushroom Soup

½ cup barley
½ cup dried lima beans
2 13¾-ounce cans Pritikin chicken broth
4 cups water
1 bay leaf
1 carrot, sliced
2 stalks celery, sliced
2 cups fresh mushrooms, sliced
1 teaspoon thyme
1 tablespoon dried parsley
¼ teaspoon pepper

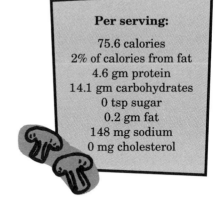

Per serving:

75.6 calories
2% of calories from fat
4.6 gm protein
14.1 gm carbohydrates
0 tsp sugar
0.2 gm fat
148 mg sodium
0 mg cholesterol

In a large strainer rinse and pick over the barley and lima beans. In a large soup pot bring the chicken broth and water to a boil. Add the barley, beans, and bay leaf. Cover and simmer for 2 hours.

Add the carrots, celery, mushrooms, thyme, parsley, and pepper. Continue simmering for 30 minutes. Remove the bay leaf and serve.

Serves 10.

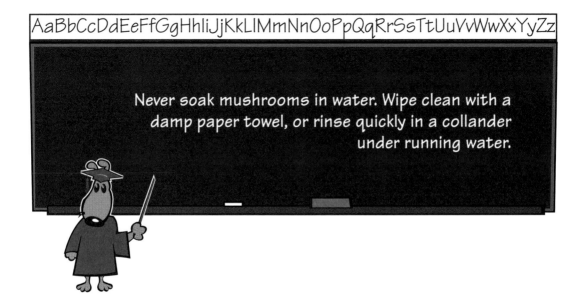

AaBbCcDdEeFfGgHhIiJjKkLlMmNnOoPpQqRrSsTtUuVvWwXxYyZz

Never soak mushrooms in water. Wipe clean with a damp paper towel, or rinse quickly in a collander under running water.

Vegetable-Rice Soup

2 teaspoons olive oil
½ cup diced onions
1 teaspoon minced garlic
½ cup sliced carrots
½ cup sliced zucchini
1 cup cut green beans
1 13¾-ounce can Pritikin beef broth
2 cups water
1 16-ounce can no-salt-added tomatoes, chopped and
    liquid reserved
¼ teaspoon oregano
¼ teaspoon basil
¼ teaspoon celery seed
¼ teaspoon tarragon
⅛ teaspoon marjoram
⅛ teaspoon rosemary
⅛ teaspoon thyme
⅛ teaspoon pepper
½ cup shredded green cabbage
2 cups cooked rice
1 tablespoon low-sodium soy sauce

Per serving:

190 calories
13% of calories from fat
13 gm protein
32.4 gm carbohydrates
0 tsp sugar
2.7 gm fat
120.2 mg sodium
11.2 mg cholesterol

In a large nonstick skillet heat the oil over medium heat. Sauté the onion and garlic in the oil until tender. Add the carrots, zucchini, and green beans, and cook for 5 minutes. Add the broth, 1 cup of water, the tomatoes, and seasonings. Cover, reduce the heat, and simmer for 10 minutes. Add the cabbage and reserved tomato juice, and simmer 5 more minutes.

Add the rice just before serving, and warm thoroughly. Add the soy sauce and serve.

Serves 6.

White (Cauliflower) Soup

6 green onions, thinly sliced
2 teaspoons olive oil
4 cups cauliflower flowerettes
1 13¾-ounce can Pritikin chicken broth
 (or 2 cups skim milk)
½ cup green peas
⅛ teaspoon pepper
½ cup plain nonfat yogurt

Per servings:

95 calories
16% of calories from fat
7.3 gm protein
15.7 gm carbohydrates
0 tsp sugar
1.7 gm fat
145 mg sodium
1.3 mg cholesterol

Steam the cauliflower for 7 to 9 minutes, or until just tender. While steaming the cauliflower, sauté the green onions in the olive oil for 3 minutes.

In a blender or food processor purée the cauliflower and onions. Pour into a saucepan. Add the broth and bring to a boil over medium low heat. Cover and simmer over very low heat for 5 minutes, stirring occasionally.

Stir in the peas and pepper. Replace the cover and remove from the heat. Let stand for 5 minutes. Stir in the yogurt and serve.

Serves 6.

Some ideas for removing fat from soups, broths, and stews:

- Spoon visible fat from the soup while it is cooking and afterward.

- Pour the liquid into a bowl. Add ice cubes, and the fat will rise to the top. Spoon off the fat, and remove the ice cubes before they dilute the flavor. Reheat the liquid before serving.

- Float a paper towel on top of the liquid for a few minutes. The towel will absorb some of the fat, and the rest will be visible to remove with a spoon.

- Pour the liquid through a coffee filter or a gravy strainer.

Lentil Stew

A great vegetarian meal. We enjoy it on cold winter nights. Reheats nicely for lunch the next day.

½ cup dry lentils
7 cups water
2 medium potatoes, peeled and cubed
1 large carrot, thinly sliced
1 medium onion, chopped
½ head green cabbage, shredded
2 tablespoons low-sodium soy sauce
½ teaspoon ginger
½ teaspoon thyme
¼ teaspoon black pepper
1 bay leaf
½ teaspoon Mrs. Dash

Per serving:

75 calories
2% of calories from fat
3.6 gm protein
15.2 gm carbohydrates
0 tsp sugar
.23 gm fat
113.7 mg sodium
0 mg cholesterol

In a large soup pan combine all of the ingredients. Bring to a boil. Reduce the heat to medium low, cover, and simmer for 1 hour and 30 minutes, stirring occasionally.
Serves 10.

The 7 basic guidelines to promote health are:

• *Eat a variety of foods.*

• *Maintain a desirable weight.*

• *Avoid too much fat, saturated fat, and cholesterol.*

• *Eat foods with adequate starch and fiber.*

• *Avoid eating too much sugar.*

• *Avoid excess sodium.*

• *Drink alcoholic beverages in moderation.*

Chicken and Okra Stew

8 ounces chicken breast, skinned and deboned,
  cut in 1-inch squares
2 13¾-ounce cans Pritikin chicken broth
1 medium onion, chopped
½ clove garlic, minced
1 14½-ounce can no-salt-added stewed tomatoes
1 10-ounce package frozen sliced okra
¼ teaspoon basil
½ teaspoon Mrs. Dash
2 cups cooked white rice

Per serving:

159 calories
12% of calories from fat
15.3 gm protein
20.2 gm carbohydrates
0 tsp sugar
2.1 gm fat
131.5 mg sodium
29.3 mg cholesterol

In a large soup pot or Dutch oven combine the chicken and broth. Bring to a boil. Cover, reduce the heat, and simmer for 3 minutes.

Add the remaining ingredients except the rice to the stew pot and bring to a boil. Cover, reduce the heat, and simmer an additional 10 minutes, stirring occasionally.

Serve the stew over rice.

Serves 6.

Salad dressing facts

Look for a good low-fat salad dressing. Regular dressings get as much as 90% of their calories from fat. Choose dressings that have no more than 2 grams of fat in a 2 tablespoon serving (1 ounce). If the dressing has nutritional information, double the numbers shown since most list a 1 tablespoon serving, and people usually use 2 tablespoons. Also, choose dressings that list water or anything but oil as the first ingredient.

Christmas Greens

Happy holidays or any days. We have enjoyed this salad at
Thanksgiving dinner. It is light and easy.

1 head Bibb lettuce
8 leaves romaine lettuce
8 leaves Belgian endive
8 leaves curly endive
½ red pepper, sliced
½ green pepper, sliced
8 cherry tomatoes
⅓ cup plain nonfat yogurt
1 tablespoon milk
1 tablespoon lemon juice
1 tablespoon prepared mustard
¼ teaspoon Dijon mustard

Per serving:

50 calories
10% of calories from fat
3.1 gm protein
10.3 gm carbohydrates
0 tsp sugar
0.6 gm fat
53.7 mg sodium
1.7 mg cholesterol

Rinse the lettuce and endive well, and spin dry in a salad spinner. Tear the leaves
into bite-sized pieces and divide among 8 salad plates. Top each with red and green
pepper rings and a cherry tomato.

In a jar with a tight-fitting lid combine the remaining ingredients. Cover and
shake well. Drizzle the dressing over each salad.

Serves 8.

Corn Salad

1 16-ounce package no-salt-added frozen corn
1¼ cups water
1 4-ounce jar diced pimiento, drained and rinsed
4 green onions, sliced
½ green pepper, diced
1 7½-ounce can hearts of palm, rinsed, drained, and
  cut into ¼-inch circles
3 tablespoons white wine vinegar
1 teaspoon tarragon
1 teaspoon dried mustard

Per serving:

60 calories
10% of calories from fat
2.6 gm protein
13.2 gm carbohydrates
0 tsp sugar
0.7 gm fat
73.5 mg sodium
0 mg cholesterol

Cook the corn in the water according to the package directions, and cool in the liquid. Drain the corn and reserve the liquid.

In a 2-quart airtight plastic container with sealing lid, combine all of the vegetables. In a small bowl combine 1 cup of cooking liquid, the vinegar, tarragon, and mustard. Pour over the salad mixture. Refrigerate for 4 hours.

Keeps for 2 to 3 days in the refrigerator.

Serves 8.

Check the label!

Low-calorie oil-free dressings are often higher in sodium than the usual bottled dressings. These dressings may be diluted with fruit juice, sodium-free chicken broth, or sodium-free tomato juice. It helps to look for dressings that have fewer than 300 mg of sodium in a 2 tablespoon serving. Remember to double the figures shown on the label, as they provide information for a 1 tablespoon serving.

Creamy Cucumber Salad

1 cucumber, peeled and seeded
¼ green pepper, diced
3 green onions, white part only, thinly sliced
½ teaspoon dill weed
Dash pepper
½ cup plain nonfat yogurt
2 tablespoons frozen unsweetened
   apple juice concentrate

Per serving:

33 calories
0% of calories from fat
1.7 gm protein
6 gm carbohydrates
0 tsp sugar
0 gm fat
22.5 mg sodium
0.1 mg cholesterol

On a paper towel squeeze the peeled and seeded cucumber dry before slicing. Cut the cucumber in half, then slice thinly. In a plastic container with an airtight cover, combine the cucumber, green pepper, and sliced green onions. Add the dill weed and sprinkle lightly with pepper. Toss gently with a fork.

   In a small bowl blend the yogurt and apple juice. Add the yogurt mixture to the cucumber mixture, stirring gently. Cover and chill for 1 hour.

   Serves 4.

Green Salad

Serve with your favorite low-fat dressing.

1/2 head lettuce
1/2 head red leaf lettuce
1 tomato, diced
2 green onions, white parts only, thinly sliced
1 stalk celery, diced
1 carrot, thinly sliced
8 cucumber slices, halved

Per serving:

23 calories
4% of calories from fat
0.7 gm protein
3.6 gm carbohydrates
0 tsp sugar
0.1 gm fat
16.8 mg sodium
0 mg cholesterol

Rinse the lettuce clean under cold water. Spin dry in a salad spinner. Add the remaining ingredients.
   Serves 6.

Pasta and Vegetable Salad

My daughter, Hilary, would take this salad to school for lunch every day if I would let her! Try pasta in different shapes for variety.

7 ounces macaroni, cooked, rinsed, and drained
1½ cups small broccoli flowerettes, steamed for
** 5 minutes**
1 cup coarsely grated carrots
1 cup thinly sliced zucchini (cut the slices in half)
¼ cup Parmesan cheese
¼ cup diced red onions (or 2 green onions, sliced)
6 black olives, sliced
½ cup Newman's Own Italian dressing
½ cup Pritikin No Oil Italian Dressing

Per serving:

68 calories
39% of calories from fat
2.2 gm protein
8.4 gm carbohydrates
0.2 tsp sugar
3.0 gm fat
196.4 mg sodium
1.6 mg cholesterol

In a large plastic container with an airtight lid combine all of the ingredients. Cover and toss until combined. Chill for several hours, stirring occasionally.
   This will keep in the refrigerator for 3 to 4 days.
   Serves 10.

Add sparkle to salads

To make salads more interesting, vary the greens and lettuces you use. In addition to the usual iceberg, Romaine, and Boston lettuces, look for arugula, Bibb, red leaf, and others. Combine the lettuces with other greens and raw vegetables such as watercress, spinach, parsley, scallions, broccoli, cauliflower buds, green beans, snow peas, sugar snap peas, sweet red pepper, and cherry tomatoes, to name a few.

Potato Salad

3 pounds red potatoes
2 eggs
4 green onions, white parts only, thinly sliced
2 stalks celery, diced
½ small green pepper, diced
½ cucumber, peeled, seeded, and diced
1 tablespoon dried flakes
1 teaspoon Mrs. Dash
½ teaspoon Italian seasoning
Dash black pepper
⅔ cup plain nonfat yogurt
1 tablespoon tarragon vinegar
1 tablespoon frozen unsweetened apple juice concentrate
2 teaspoons salt-free Dijon mustard
½ teaspoon celery seed
Paprika

Per serving:

71 calories
2% of calories from fat
4.1 gm protein
13.7 gm carbohydrates
0 tsp sugar
0.2 gm fat
126.7 mg sodium
0 mg cholesterol

About 8 hours before serving, prepare the salad. In a large pot filled with water, boil the potatoes with skins on until tender when pierced with a fork. Allow to cool, then peel and dice.

Place the eggs in a separate saucepan filled with cold water. Bring to a boil over medium high heat. Reduce the heat and simmer for 25 minutes. Run cold water over the eggs, then cool in the refrigerator. When cool, peel the eggs and slice in half. Discard the egg yolks, then grate the egg whites.

About 6 hours before serving, make the salad. Combine the potatoes, eggs, and the next 8 ingredients in a 2-quart airtight plastic container. In a 2-cup liquid measure combine the next 5 ingredients. Stir well, then pour over the potato mixture. Toss gently with a fork. Cover with the airtight top and chill for 4 to 6 hours for the flavors to combine. Serve topped with a dash of paprika. The leftovers will keep for 2 to 3 days in the refrigerator.

Serves 8.

Popeye's Spinach Salad

We always sing "Popeye the Sailor Man" when serving this salad!

2 eggs
3 cups fresh spinach, torn in bite-sized pieces
1 cup fresh bean sprouts
1 cup sliced fresh mushrooms
2 green onions, sliced
4 tablespoons bottled low-fat French dressing (or Western)

Per serving:

53 calories
25% of calories from fat
4.1 gm protein
8 gm carbohydrates
0.6 tsp sugar
1.2 gm fat
184.1 mg sodium
0 mg cholesterol

About 4 hours before cooking, place the eggs in a small saucepan with cool water. Bring to a boil over medium high heat. Reduce the heat and simmer gently for 25 minutes. Run cold water over the eggs to cool, then refrigerate until ready to use for salad.

Discard the egg yolks and chop the egg whites. In a salad bowl combine the chopped egg and remaining ingredients, tossing gently. Top with salad dressing and enjoy.

Serves 4.

Yogurt Cheese Fruit Dip

½ cup Yogurt Cheese (see recipe, p. 66)
2 tablespoons pineapple juice concentrate, thawed
1 tablespoon white wine vinegar
1 tablespoon honey
1 teaspoon poppy seeds
½ teaspoon vanilla extract
1 apple, cored and sliced
1 pear, cored and sliced

Per serving:

69 calories
11% of calories from fat
2.4 gm protein
14.3 gm carbohydrates
0 tsp sugar
.83 gm fat
24 mg sodium
0 mg cholesterol

Combine the first 6 ingredients. Stir well. Serve with sliced apple and pear or the fruit of your choice!

Serves 6.

Spinach Salad with Poppy Seed Dressing

3 tablespoons water
1 teaspoon cornstarch
2 tablespoons white rice vinegar
1 tablespoon honey
2 teaspoons Dijon mustard
⅔ cup unsweetened orange juice
¾ teaspoon poppy seeds
¼ pound fresh spinach
1 unpeeled red pear, cored and cubed
1 11-ounce can mandarin oranges, drained
½ cup alfalfa sprouts
¼ cup raisins
3 tablespoons slivered almonds

Per serving:

144 calories
15% of calories from fat
2.8 gm protein
31.4 gm carbohydrates
0 tsp sugar
2.4 gm fat
53.8 mg sodium
0 mg cholesterol

In a jar with a tight-fitting lid combine the water and cornstarch. Cover and shake vigorously until the cornstarch is dissolved. In a saucepan combine the cornstarch mixture, vinegar, honey, mustard, and orange juice. Bring to a boil over medium high heat, stirring constantly, until slightly thickened. Remove from the heat. Pour into a small bowl, add the poppy seeds, and chill.

Wash the spinach thoroughly, removing the stems and tearing the leaves into bite-sized pieces. Arrange the spinach in 4 salad bowls. Divide each of the next 5 ingredients among the salad bowls.

Pour 1 tablespoon of dressing over each salad. Refrigerate remaining dressing. Serves 4.

Vinegar adds zip

Use a little vinegar to pep up stews, barbecued chicken and meats, fish, mixed vegetables, and salads. A tablespoon of cider or wine vinegar adds a lot of flavor but only 2 or 3 calories. You can alter the taste or color of a recipe simply by using a different vinegar.

Sweet Yellow Slaw

1½ cups shredded green cabbage
1 cup shredded carrots
½ cup raisins
2 tablespoons toasted almond slivers
½ cup vanilla nonfat yogurt
1 8-ounce can unsweetened pineapple tidbits, drained

Combine the ingredients in a bowl and serve.
  Serves 4.

Per serving:

132 calories
14% of calories from fat
3.4 gm protein
27.9 gm carbohydrates
0 tsp sugar
2.1 gm fat
41.4 mg sodium
0.1 mg cholesterol

Tomato-Asparagus Salad

1 pound fresh asparagus
1 teaspoon Italian dressing (Newman's Own)
2 plum tomatoes, thinly sliced
2 hard-cooked egg whites, chopped

Snap the ends off the asparagus. Steam for 5 to 7
minutes, until tender but still crisp. Rinse under cold
water. Place in a container with an airtight lid and
drizzle with Italian dressing. Cover and place in
the refrigerator to cool, approximately 20 minutes
to 1 hour.
  Arrange the chilled asparagus on 4 salad plates.
Top with tomatoes and chopped egg whites.
  Serves 4.

Per serving:

31 calories
5% of calories from fat
3.5 gm protein
4.2 gm carbohydrates
0 tsp sugar
0.2 gm fat
35.7 mg sodium
0 mg cholesterol

Easter Bunny Salad

Children love to help make their own bunnies.

4 lettuce leaves, washed and dried
1 14-ounce can unsweetened Bartlett pear halves
8 raisins
8 almonds
4 tablespoons low-fat cottage cheese

Place a lettuce leaf on each of 4 salad plates. Place a pear upside down on each plate. Use 2 raisins for the eyes, 2 almonds for the bunny's ears, and 1 tablespoon of cottage cheese for the tail.
   Serves 4.

Per serving:

138 calories
17% of calories from fat
3.2 gm protein
28.8 gm carbohydrates
0 tsp sugar
2.6 gm fat
59.8 mg sodium
0.6 mg cholesterol

Fruit Delight

Easy to make. Little ones can help by slicing the bananas.

1 11-ounce can mandarin oranges
2 cups strawberry halves
1 cup sliced bananas
½ cup diced apples
1 cup small marshmallows

Drain the oranges, reserving liquid. In a large bowl combine all of the ingredients except the marshmallows. Add liquid from the oranges and toss. Cover and chill for 1 hour.
   Add the marshmallows and toss gently. Serve immediately.
   Serves 6.

Per serving:

102 calories
4% of calories from fat
1.2 gm protein
25.6 gm carbohydrates
1.5 tsp sugar
0.5 gm fat
3.7 mg sodium
0 mg cholesterol

Fresh Fruit Salad

This salad is a touch healthier than the preceding one—but not as popular with young ones because there are no marshmallows.

1 banana, sliced
1 Red Delicious apple, diced
1 cup sliced strawberries
½ cup seedless grapes, sliced
1 tablespoon lemon juice
1 6-ounce carton plain nonfat yogurt
2 tablespoons frozen unsweetened apple
   juice concentrate
1 tablespoon honey

Per serving:

74 calories
4% of calories from fat
1.9 gm protein
17.5 gm carbohydrates
0 tsp sugar
0.3 gm fat
21.4 mg sodium
0.1 mg cholesterol

In a glass bowl combine the fruit. Sprinkle with lemon juice to retard browning. In another bowl combine the remaining ingredients. Divide the fruit among 6 salad bowls, topping with dressing. Serve immediately.
   Serves 6.

Hawaiian Fruit Salad

¼ cup honey
2 tablespoons white wine vinegar
1 tablespoon water
¼ teaspoon lemon rind
1½ cups sliced strawberries
¾ cup sliced banana
½ cup canned unsweetened pineapple chunks
1 papaya, peeled, seeded, and chopped
1 large kiwi, peeled and sliced

Per serving:

156 calories
4% of calories from fat
1.5 gm protein
40 gm carbohydrates
0 tsp sugar
0.7 gm fat
4.3 mg sodium
0 mg cholesterol

In a jar with a tight-fitting lid combine the first 4 ingredients. Cover and shake until well blended. Refrigerate until chilled.
   Combine the fruit in a bowl and toss gently. Divide the fruit mixture among 4 salad plates. Top with dressing.
   Serves 4.

Rise and Shine

Little ones can make this salad on their own, if a parent opens the can of pineapple.

¼ cup plain nonfat yogurt
1 teaspoon honey
4 slices pineapple

In a small bowl combine the yogurt and honey. Place 1 slice of pineapple in each of 4 bowls. Put a tablespoon of the yogurt mixture in the middle of each pineapple.
   Serves 4.

Per serving:
25 calories
4% of calories from fat
0.7 gm protein
5.9 gm carbohydrates
0 tsp sugar
0.1 gm fat
8.4 mg sodium
0 mg cholesterol

Summer Fruit Salad

1 8-ounce carton orange nonfat yogurt
1 tablespoon lemon juice
1 teaspoon poppy seeds
1 teaspoon grated orange rind
1 cup fresh blueberries
½ cup sliced bananas (about 1)
1 cup peeled and sliced peaches (about 1)
6 lettuce leaves, rinsed and dried

Per serving:
62 calories
0% of calories from fat
2.8 gm protein
12.8 gm carbohydrates
0 tsp sugar
0 gm fat
27.6 mg sodium
5 mg cholesterol

In a small bowl combine the first 4 ingredients. Cover and refrigerate until chilled.
   In a medium bowl gently toss the fruit together. Arrange the lettuce on 6 salad plates. Place the fruit on top of the lettuce and place a dollop of dressing on each serving.
   Serves 6.

Waldorf Salad

This salad is great for holidays as well as summertime meals.

½ cup water
2 tablespoons lemon juice
2 ripe Bosc pears, cored and cut into ½-inch cubes
2 Granny Smith apples, cored and cubed
2 stalks celery, cut in half lengthwise,
    then into ¼-inch slices
2 carrots, peeled and cut into ¼-inch slices
½ cup coarsely chopped walnuts
1 cup raisins
1 cup vanilla nonfat yogurt
½ cup cholesterol-free nonfat mayonnaise
1 tablespoon chopped fresh mint

Per serving:

140 calories
21% of calories from fat
2.7 gm protein
27.9 gm carbohydrates
0 tsp sugar
3.2 gm fat
183.9 mg sodium
0.5 mg cholesterol

In a large mixing bowl combine the water and lemon juice. Stir in the pears and apples, tossing gently until completely coated with liquid. Set aside for 10 minutes.

Drain the liquid from the fruit. Add the celery, carrots, walnuts, and raisins, and toss gently. In a small bowl combine the yogurt and mayonnaise. Pour over the salad mixture and toss until all of the ingredients are well mixed. Cover and refrigerate for 1 hour. Before serving, mix well and sprinkle with mint.

Serves 12.

Favorite Fruited Chicken Salad

This recipe is a summer favorite of my sister-in-law, Joan Schrader, a great cook in her own right.

¾ **pound diced, cooked chicken breast**
1 **cup diced celery**
1 **cup orange sections, cut in bite-sized pieces**
1 **cup unsweetened pineapple tidbits, drained**
2 **tablespoons canola oil**
2 **tablespoons freshly squeezed orange juice**
2 **tablespoons white vinegar**
½ **cup plain nonfat yogurt (or cholesterol-free nonfat**
 mayonnaise)
Lettuce leaves
½ **cup slivered almonds**

Per serving:
198 calories
30% of calories from fat
18.1 gm protein
16.3 gm carbohydrates
1.3 tsp sugar
6.8 gm fat
75 mg sodium
44.4 mg cholesterol

In a large plastic bowl with a cover, combine the first 4 ingredients. In a separate container combine the oil, orange juice, and vinegar, mixing well. Cover the chicken mixture with marinade, stirring until thoroughly coated. Refrigerate for 1 hour.

Drain off the remaining marinade. Toss the chicken mixture with yogurt. Serve on lettuce leaves and top with almonds.

Serves 6.

AaBbCcDdEeFfGgHhIiJjKkLlMmNnOoPpQqRrSsTtUuVvWwXxYyZz

Reduce the calorie content of commercial fruited yogurt by choosing the fruit-on-the-bottom type and removing one-half to two-thirds of the fruit mixture before blending. This removes 50 to 75 calories. Commercial fruited yogurts are high in sugar, but low in vitamins A and C.

Pasta and Chicken Salad

3 cups uncooked pasta (bow ties, spirals, wheels, etc.)
1 tomato, diced
1 teaspoon basil
¼ teaspoon Mrs. Dash
Dash cayenne pepper
Dash garlic powder
3 tablespoons white wine vinegar
2 teaspoons olive oil
PAM baking spray
2 tablespoons white wine
½ pound boneless chicken, cut into bite-sized pieces
½ cup chopped green bell pepper
½ cup chopped onion
1 tablespoon grated Parmesan cheese

Per serving:

173 calories
19% of calories from fat
14.3 gm protein
19.4 gm carbohydrates
0 tsp sugar
3.6 gm fat
43.9 mg sodium
30.0 mg cholesterol

Cook the pasta according to package directions, omitting salt and oil. (Never cook pasta with salt or oil. It is not needed.) Drain and set aside.

In a small bowl, combine the tomatoes, seasonings, vinegar, and oil. Set aside.

Coat a large nonstick skillet with baking spray. Heat the wine over medium high heat. Add the chicken and brown for 5 minutes. Add the green pepper and onion and continue cooking until the chicken is done. Add the cooked pasta and the tomato mixture to the chicken. Toss well. Serve topped with Parmesan cheese.

Serves 6.

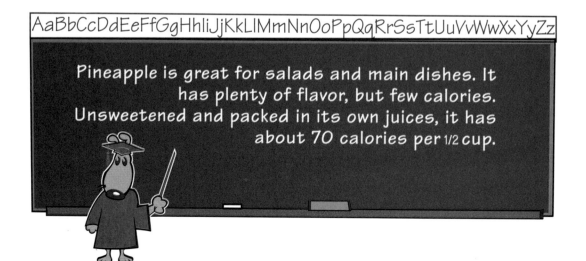

AaBbCcDdEeFfGgHhIiJjKkLlMmNnOoPpQqRrSsTtUuVvWwXxYyZz

Pineapple is great for salads and main dishes. It has plenty of flavor, but few calories. Unsweetened and packed in its own juices, it has about 70 calories per 1/2 cup.

Sweet Chicken and Fruit Salad

We enjoy this meal as a summer treat. It is light and refreshing and is perfect served with your favorite muffins.

½ cup raspberry vinegar
¼ cup honey
1 tablespoon olive oil
1 teaspoon lemon juice
2 cups honeydew melon balls
2 cups cantaloupe balls
8 ounces boneless, skinless chicken
   breast, cut into bite-sized pieces
1 head red leaf lettuce
½ cup fresh raspberries

Per serving:

323 calories
11% of calories from fat
19.6 gm protein
58.3 gm carbohydrates
0 tsp sugar
4.1 gm fat
146.2 mg sodium
40.0 mg cholesterol

In a jar with a tight-fitting lid combine the vinegar, honey, oil, and lemon juice. Cover and shake to mix thoroughly.

In a 1-quart plastic container with a lid, combine the honeydew and cantaloupe balls. Pour ½ of the vinegar mixture over the fruit. Cover tightly and chill.

In a separate 1-quart plastic container with a lid, arrange the chicken. Pour the remaining vinegar mixture over the chicken and marinate for 30 minutes in the refrigerator.

Drain the marinade from the chicken. Microwave on high for 3 to 4 minutes, stirring twice or until the chicken is cooked. Drain the vinegar from the fruit. Rinse and spin dry the lettuce leaves. Arrange 2 lettuce leaves on each of 4 plates. Place ¼ of the chicken on each plate. Place 1 cup of melon balls over each serving of chicken and top with 2 tablespoons raspberries.

Serves 4.

Chicken Salad with Couscous

A good luncheon or light dinner dish, especially in the summertime heat.

1½ cups diced cooked chicken breast, skin removed
1 cup couscous, cooked and cooled
2 stalks celery, sliced
1 20-ounce can unsweetened pineapple chunks, drained
¼ cup diced green pepper
2 tablespoons diced pimiento
½ cup plain nonfat yogurt
¼ cup cholesterol-free nonfat mayonnaise
1 tablespoon lemon juice
½ teaspoon curry powder
Dash black pepper

Per serving:

225 calories
9% of calories from fat
17.7 gm protein
33.2 gm carbohydrates
0 tsp sugar
2.1 gm fat
205 mg sodium
37.1 mg cholesterol

In a plastic container with an airtight lid, combine the first 5 ingredients. In a small bowl combine the remaining ingredients, mixing well. Pour the dressing over the chicken mixture and toss gently with a fork. Refrigerate for 2 hours.

Serve on a lettuce leaf.

Serves 6.

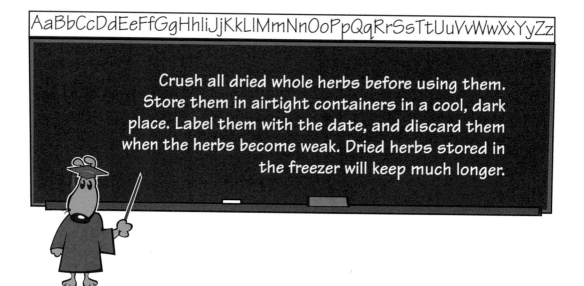

AaBbCcDdEeFfGgHhIiJjKkLlMmNnOoPpQqRrSsTtUuVvWwXxYyZz

Crush all dried whole herbs before using them. Store them in airtight containers in a cool, dark place. Label them with the date, and discard them when the herbs become weak. Dried herbs stored in the freezer will keep much longer.

Turkey Chef's Salad

A great summertime meal. Serve in large bowls or on dinner plates with warmed French bread.

1 cup sliced carrots
1 cup cauliflower flowerettes
5 ounces frozen artichoke hearts
1 cup frozen Italian green beans (or fresh broccoli or asparagus)
2 green onions, chopped
¼ pound fresh mushrooms, sliced
½ cup Pritikin No Oil Italian Dressing
1 tablespoon olive oil
1 head romaine lettuce
1 cup frozen peas
1 6-ounce sliced deli turkey breast,
  cut into 1-inch squares
1 tomato, cut into chunks

Per serving:

114 calories
20% of calories from fat
11.9 gm protein
11.8 gm carbohydrates
0.1 tsp sugar
2.5 gm fat
168.8 mg sodium
20 mg cholesterol

In a steamer steam the carrots, cauliflower, and artichokes for 4 to 5 minutes. After they have begun to soften, add the frozen beans. Steam for another 2 to 3 minutes, taking care that vegetables are only crunchy, not mushy. Remove from the steamer to a colander and cool.

In a 2-quart airtight plastic container, combine the cooled vegetables, onions, and mushrooms. Pour the salad dressing and olive oil over the vegetable mixture, then toss gently with a fork. Cover the mixture tightly and refrigerate for 1 to 2 hours.

About 15 minutes before serving, wash the lettuce and tear it into bite-sized pieces. Spin dry in a salad spinner. Place the lettuce in a medium salad bowl. Top with the peas, turkey, and tomato chunks. Pour the vegetable mixture over the salad and toss, combining well.

Serves 6.

Tuna Pasta Salad

1 7-ounce package tricolor corkscrew pasta, cooked,
  rinsed, and drained
1 cup frozen corn, thawed
1 2-ounce jar diced pimiento, drained
¼ cup diced red onion
1 6-ounce low-sodium water-packed tuna, drained
1 cup diced cucumbers
½ cup plain nonfat yogurt
⅛ cup cholesterol-free nonfat mayonnaise
⅛ teaspoon pepper
¼ teaspoon paprika

Per serving:

98 calories
22% of calories from fat
8.7 gm protein
10.6 gm carbohydrates
0 tsp sugar
2.4 gm fat
58.4 mg sodium
15 mg cholesterol

In a large bowl combine the first 6 ingredients, mixing well. In a small bowl combine the remaining ingredients, stirring well. Pour the dressing over the salad and toss well. Cover and chill for at least 2 hours.

Serves 8.

AaBbCcDdEeFfGgHhIiJjKkLlMmNnOoPpQqRrSsTtUuVvWwXxYyZz

Rinsing all types of water-packed tuna and beans in running water for 1 minute reduces the sodium. The sodium in water-packed tuna rinsed for 1 minute drops from 418 mg to around 74 mg. Rinsing canned green beans for 1 minute removes about 40% of the sodium.

Tuna Rice Salad

A great summer meal.

1 cup long-grain white rice
2 cups water
2 tablespoons chopped onion
1 medium carrot, thinly sliced
1 cup frozen green peas, thawed
⅛ teaspoon pepper
1 6-ounce can low-sodium water-packed tuna, chilled
½ cup chopped cucumber
½ cup cholesterol-free nonfat mayonnaise
½ cup plain nonfat yogurt
½ cup skim milk
Lettuce leaves (optional)

Per serving:

219 calories
3% of calories from fat
19.5 gm protein
32.2 gm carbohydrates
0 tsp sugar
0.8 gm fat
137.6 mg sodium
32.1 mg cholesterol

Cook the rice in the water according to the package directions. Five minutes before the rice is finished cooking, add the onions and carrots. Remove from the heat and add the peas. Let the mixture stand for 5 minutes. Chill.

Combine the remaining ingredients and stir into the rice mixture. Place each serving on a lettuce leaf.

Serves 4.

Mexican Taco Salad

½ pound very lean ground beef (Naturlite)
½ cup chopped onion
1 15-ounce can black beans, drained and rinsed
½ cup mild salsa (see recipe, page 64)
2 cups shredded iceberg lettuce
2 tomatoes, chopped
½ cup grated Kraft Reduced-Fat Monterey Jack Cheese
1 ripe avocado, sliced
½ cup Pritikin French dressing
1 cup broken lightly salted blue corn tortilla chips

Per serving:

241 calories
38% of calories from fat
10.3 gm protein
28.1 gm carbohydrates
0.8 tsp sugar
10.2 gm fat
230 mg sodium
12 mg cholesterol

In a large nonstick frying pan brown the ground beef and onion, cooking until there is no pinkness left in the meat. Add the beans and salsa, cover, and simmer for 10 minutes.

Tear the lettuce into bite-sized pieces and dry in a salad spinner. Place the lettuce in a large salad bowl, and add the tomatoes, cheese, and avocado. Toss lightly. Add the hot beef mixture and salad dressing, and toss well.

Serve on large plates, and top with crumbled tortilla chips. Additional salsa may be provided at the table.

Serves 6.

Muffins
and
Breads

Apple Muffins

PAM baking spray
⅔ cup plus 1 tablespoon all-purpose flour
⅛ cup whole-wheat flour
1 tablespoon wheat germ
1 tablespoon soya flour
1 tablespoon nonfat powdered milk
1 cup Quaker Old-Fashioned Oats
⅛ cup brown sugar
1 tablespoon low-sodium baking powder (Featherweight)
1 teaspoon cinnamon
⅔ cup skim milk
⅛ cup apple juice
2 egg whites, lightly beaten
¼ cup safflower oil
1 apple, peeled and chopped

Per muffin:
135 calories
27% of calories from fat
3.5 gm protein
21.5 gm carbohydrates
1.5 tsp sugar
4.1 gm fat
20.5 mg sodium
0.3 mg cholesterol

Spray 12 muffin cups with baking spray. In a large bowl combine the dry ingredients.

In a separate bowl beat together the milk, apple juice, egg whites, and oil. Pour the liquid ingredients into the dry ingredients, stirring just until moistened. Fold in the apples. Spoon the batter into the prepared cups, filling each ⅔ full. Bake at 400° for 20 to 22 minutes.

Makes 12 muffins.

Blueberry Muffins

A real favorite at our house, and a good school snack, too.

PAM baking spray
2¼ cups whole-wheat flour
¼ cup oat bran
1¼ teaspoons baking soda
2 egg whites, lightly beaten
⅓ cup honey
¼ cup safflower oil
1¾ cups buttermilk
2 cups frozen unsweetened blueberries

> **Per muffin:**
>
> 96 calories
> 24% of calories from fat
> 3.0 gm protein
> 16.5 gm carbohydrates
> 0 tsp sugar
> 2.6 gm fat
> 99.8 mg sodium
> 0.8 mg cholesterol

Spray 20 muffin cups with baking spray. In a large bowl combine the dry ingredients. In a separate bowl beat together the egg whites, honey, oil, and buttermilk. Pour the liquid ingredients into the dry ingredients, stirring just until moistened. Fold in the blueberries. Spoon the mixture into the prepared cups, filling each ⅔ full. Bake at 400° for 15 to 20 minutes, until lightly browned.

Makes 20 muffins.

Fiber and fats

Whole-wheat bread and all whole-grain foods, along with many fruits and vegetables, contain insoluble fiber, thought to protect against colon cancer.

Fruits, vegetables, and whole grains are good sources of complex carbohydrates. Soluble fiber, found in oat bran, beans, cereals, fruits, and vegetables, can lower cholesterol.

Use polyunsaturated and monounsaturated fats such as corn oil, olive oil, and safflower oil instead of butter and lard.

Sweet Blueberry Muffins

These blueberry muffins are much sweeter than the other recipe. We often have these for a treat or dessert, but they can be served with a meal. The leftovers are great for snacks and are freezable, too.

PAM baking spray
2 egg whites, slightly beaten
⅛ cup corn oil
¼ cup sugar
¼ cup maple syrup
1½ cups skim milk
1½ cups all-purpose flour
½ cup whole-wheat flour
1½ tablespoons low-sodium baking
    powder (Featherweight)
½ cup wheat or oat bran
1½ cups frozen unsweetened blueberries

> **Per muffin:**
>
> 168 calories
> 27% of calories from fat
> 4.2 gm fat
> 27.3 gm carbohydrates
> 1.8 tsp sugar
> 5 gm fat
> 28.2 mg sodium
> 0.5 mg cholesterol

Line 12 large muffin cups with paper liners or spray with baking spray. In a large bowl combine the egg whites, oil, sugar, syrup, and milk. In a medium bowl combine the flours and the baking powder. With a fork stir the dry ingredients into the liquid, blending just until moistened. Fold in the bran and blueberries. Spoon the batter into the prepared cups, filling each full. Bake at 375° for 25 minutes or until lightly browned. Cool on a wire rack.

 Makes 12 large muffins.

Widen taste horizons

Keep offering new tastes. As your child's taste buds develop, so will the interest in trying more complex flavors and a wider variety of foods.

 Shopping and cooking are activities that kids love. When they're along, discuss the fact that foods have different nutrients and calorie levels.

Cinnamon Muffins

PAM baking spray
1 cup all-purpose flour
2 teaspoons low-sodium baking powder (Featherweight)
1¾ cups skim milk
1½ cups oat bran
2 egg whites
¼ cup packed brown sugar
1½ teaspoons cinnamon
1½ tablespoons corn oil

> **Per muffin:**
>
> 95 calories
> 13% of calories from fat
> 3.7 gm protein
> 16.7 gm carbohydrates
> 1.1 tsp sugar
> 1.4 gm fat
> 35.8 mg sodium
> 0.6 mg cholesterol

Spray 12 muffin cups with baking spray. In a medium bowl combine the flour and baking powder. In a large bowl combine the milk and oat bran. Add the egg whites, brown sugar, cinnamon, and oil. Mix well. Fold the dry ingredients into the liquid, stirring just until moistened. Spoon the batter into the prepared cups, filling each ⅔ full. Bake at 350° for 20 to 25 minutes, or until nicely browned.

Makes 12 muffins.

Some fiber facts:

- *A Nature Valley Granola Bar has less fiber than a Snickers bar.*

- *A serving of Pritikin Navy Bean Soup has twice as much fiber as a serving of Kellogg's All Bran cereal.*

- *The highest fiber vegetable is a baked potato with skin.*

Christmas Muffins

These are the muffins we serve for Christmas breakfast, and we love them. If the pecans are omitted, each muffin will contain 105 calories; 26 % of calories from fat; 2.8 gm protein; 16.8 gm carbohydrates; 1.0 tsp sugar; 3 gm fat; 48.9 mg sodium; 0.3 mg cholesterol.

PAM baking spray
1 cup unbleached all-purpose flour
½ cup whole-wheat flour
½ cup finely ground pecans
¼ cup sugar
2 teaspoons ground ginger
1 tablespoon low-sodium baking powder (Featherweight)
¾ cup skim milk
2 egg whites
Finely grated peel of 2 oranges
⅓ cup freshly squeezed orange juice
½ teaspoon vanilla extract
3 tablespoons Promise margarine, melted
2 tablespoons sugar
½ teaspoon cinnamon

Per muffin:

136 calories
41% of calories from fat
32.0 gm protein
17.5 gm carbohydrates
1.0 tsp sugar
6.2 gm fat
48.9 mg sodium
0.3 mg cholesterol

Spray 12 muffin cups with baking spray. In a large bowl combine the flours, pecans, ¼ cup sugar, ginger, and baking powder. In a medium bowl combine the milk, egg whites, orange peel, orange juice, vanilla, and melted butter. Whisk until thoroughly mixed. Form a well in the center of the dry ingredients. Pour the liquid ingredients into the well, stirring with a fork until just moistened. Spoon the batter into the prepared cups, filling each ⅔ full.

In a small bowl combine the remaining 2 tablespoons of sugar and the cinnamon. Sprinkle the mixture over the muffin batter. Bake in a 425° oven for 17 to 20 minutes. Do not overcook, or they will be dry. Remove the muffins from the pan immediately and cool on a wire rack.

Makes 12 muffins.

Jelly Belly Muffins

PAM baking spray
1⅓ cup all-purpose flour
⅔ cup whole-wheat flour
1 cup uncooked oats
¼ cup packed brown sugar
1 tablespoon low-sodium baking powder (Featherweight)
½ teaspoon ground cinnamon
1⅓ cups skim milk
2 tablespoons safflower oil
2 egg whites, lightly beaten
12 teaspoons low-sugar jelly, any flavor

> **Per muffin:**
>
> 161 calories
> 20% of calories from fat
> 4.8 gm protein
> 29.3 gm carbohydrates
> 1.7 tsp sugar
> 3 gm fat
> 25.3 mg sodium
> 0.4 mg cholesterol

Spray 12 muffin cups with baking spray. In a large bowl combine the dry ingredients. In a small bowl combine the milk, oil, and egg whites. Pour the liquid ingredients into the dry ingredients, stirring just until moistened. Spoon the batter into the prepared cups, filling each ⅔ full. Gently press 1 teaspoonful of jelly into the middle of each cup of batter. Bake at 400° for 20 to 25 minutes. Remove the muffins from the pan as soon as possible and cool on a wire rack.

Watch out for hot jelly. It can burn.

Makes 12 muffins.

Encourage healthy attitudes

If you don't want your kids to snack in front of the television, you shouldn't either. If you want your kids to be accepting of imperfect bodies, you shouldn't make jokes about love handles. Giving children self-confidence can prevent an unhealthy obsession with weight.

Encourage independence by letting kids get their own snacks and occasionally pick the dinner menu. Just make sure the choices are healthy.

Nutty Raisin Muffins

PAM baking spray
2 cups oat bran
¼ cup packed brown sugar
1 tablespoon low-sodium baking powder (Featherweight)
1 cup skim milk
2 egg whites, lightly beaten
¼ cup dark molasses
1 tablespoon safflower or vegetable oil
¼ cup raisins
¼ cup walnuts

Per muffin:

95 calories
25% of calories from fat
2.9 gm protein
15.5 gm carbohydrates
1.8 tsp sugar
2.7 gm fat
35.4 mg sodium
0.3 mg cholesterol

Spray 12 muffin cups with baking spray. In a large
bowl combine the dry ingredients. In a small bowl combine the milk, egg whites,
molasses, and oil. Pour the liquid ingredients into the dry ingredients, stirring just
until moistened. Fold in the raisins and walnuts. Spoon the batter into the prepared cups, filling each ⅔ full. Bake at 400° for 13 to 15 minutes, until lightly
browned. Cool in the pan on a wire rack.
    Makes 12 muffins.

A breakdown of 1 tablespoon of some popular spreads:

- *Butter has 100 calories in a tablespoon, 7.1 gm saturated fat, 3.3 gm monounsaturated fat, 0.4 gm polyunsaturated fat, 31 mg cholesterol, and 116 mg sodium.*

- *Low-calorie margarine has 50 calories, 1.1 gm saturated fat, 2.2 gm monounsaturated fat, 1.9 gm polyunsaturated fat, no cholesterol, and 134 mg sodium.*

- *Jam has 55 calories, is low in sodium, and has no fat or cholesterol.*

- *Cream cheese has 52 calories, 3.1 gm saturated fat, 1.4 gm monounsaturated fat, 0.2 gm polyunsaturated fat, and 16 mg cholesterol.*

- *Peanut butter has 95 calories, 1.4 gm saturated fat, 4.0 gm monounsaturated fat, 2.5 gm polyunsaturated fat, no cholesterol, 5 gm protein, and 75 mg sodium.*

Pumpkin Muffins

Very appropriate for Halloween and Thanksgiving meals.

PAM baking spray
½ cup raisins
1½ cups oat bran
⅔ cup packed brown sugar
½ cup all-purpose flour
1 tablespoon low-sodium baking powder (Featherweight)
1 teaspoon pumpkin pie spice
1 cup canned pumpkin
½ cup skim milk
2 egg whites, lightly beaten
4 teaspoons corn oil

Per muffin:
128 calories
13% of calories from fat
2.7 gm protein
26.4 gm carbohydrates
3 tsp sugar
1.8 gm fat
26.1 mg sodium
0.2 mg cholesterol

Spray 12 muffin cups with baking spray. In a small bowl plump the raisins in hot water for 15 minutes. Drain. In a large bowl combine the dry ingredients. In a small bowl combine the pumpkin, milk, egg whites, and oil. Pour the liquid ingredients into the dry ingredients, stirring just until moistened. Fold in the raisins. Spoon the batter into the prepared cups, filling each ⅔ full. Bake at 425° for 18 to 20 minutes. Remove the muffins from the pan as soon as possible and cool on a wire rack.

Makes 12 muffins.

Even well-meaning comments and strategies can harm a child's eating habits. Some "Don'ts" include:

- *Don't say "Clean your plate!" Serve a variety of healthy, appealing foods, and let the child decide how much to eat, as long as the child is growing properly.*

- *Don't offer food when your child has had a rough day. Give your undivided attention, instead.*

- *Don't say "You'll spoil your appetite." Unlike adults, children need refueling about every three hours. They're asking because they have an appetite.*

- *Don't withhold dessert until the vegetables are all eaten. What the child doesn't get from the broccoli will be made up from orange juice, milk, chicken, and other meats.*

Veggie Muffins

This is one of my children's favorites.

PAM baking spray
¾ cup all-purpose flour
¼ cup oat bran
2 teaspoons low-sodium baking powder (Featherweight)
1 teaspoon baking soda
2 egg whites
¼ cup brown sugar
2 tablespoons corn oil
¾ cup skim milk
¼ cup coarsely grated zucchini
¼ cup coarsely grated carrot
¼ cup grated onion

Per muffin:

168 calories
26% of calories from fat
4.8 gm protein
26.2 gm carbohydrates
2.3 tsp sugar
4.9 gm fat
233.1 mg sodium
0.5 mg cholesterol

Spray 12 muffin cups with baking spray. In a large bowl combine the dry ingredients. In a medium bowl beat together the egg whites, brown sugar, and oil. Stir in the milk. Pour the liquid ingredients into the dry ingredients, stirring just until moistened. Fold in the vegetables. Spoon the batter into the prepared cups, filling each ⅔ full. Bake at 325° for 20 to 25 minutes, or until a toothpick inserted in the center comes out clean. Remove from the pan and cool on a wire rack.

Makes 12 muffins.

Banana Bread

If you reduce the walnuts to ⅛ cup, the percentage of calories from fat drops to 30%. If you omit the walnuts, it drops to 25%.

PAM baking spray
1½ cups whole-wheat flour
1 tablespoon low-sodium baking powder (Featherweight)
½ teaspoon baking soda
1 cup bran
¼ cup chopped walnuts
¼ cup sunflower seeds
2 egg whites, slightly beaten
¼ cup honey
¼ cup corn oil
¼ cup skim milk
3 or 4 very ripe bananas, mashed

Per slice:

130 calories
34% of calories from fat
3.5 gm protein
19.7 gm carbohydrates
0 tsp sugar
5.0 gm fat
48.4 mg sodium
0.1 mg cholesterol

Spray an 8 x 4-inch loaf pan with baking spray. In a large bowl combine the flour, baking powder, baking soda, bran, walnuts, and sunflower seeds. In a separate bowl combine the remaining ingredients. Pour the liquid ingredients into the dry ingredients and stir until well blended. Pour the batter into the prepared pan. Bake at 350° for 50 minutes to 1 hour, until nicely browned and a toothpick inserted in the center comes out clean. Cool on a wire rack.

Makes 1 loaf, or 16 slices.

AaBbCcDdEeFfGgHhIiJjKkLlMmNnOoPpQqRrSsTtUuVvWwXxYyZz

To warm bread or rolls in the microwave, cover them loosely with a dry paper towel and heat for 15 to 20 seconds at medium power. If necessary, heat for a couple of seconds longer, but take care not to overdo it or the bread will become tough.

Blueberry and Walnut Bread

PAM baking spray
1 cup all-purpose flour
¾ cup whole-wheat flour
⅔ cup packed brown sugar
2 teaspoons low-sodium baking powder (Featherweight)
½ teaspoon baking soda
Juice of 1 orange
2 tablespoons corn oil
Water
1 tablespoon grated orange peel
2 egg whites, lightly beaten
1 cup fresh or frozen blueberries
½ cup chopped walnuts
½ cup rolled oats

Per slice:

129 calories
23% of calories from fat
2.9 gm protein
2.3 gm carbohydrates
2.2 tsp sugar
3.3 gm fat
45.1 mg sodium
0 mg cholesterol

Spray an 8 x 4-inch loaf pan with baking spray. In a large bowl combine the dry ingredients. In a measuring cup measure the orange juice. Add the oil, and then add enough water to measure ¾ cup. Pour the juice mixture into the dry ingredients along with the orange peel and egg whites. Stir just until moistened.

In a small bowl toss together the blueberries, walnuts, and oats. Gently fold the mixture into the batter, taking care not to mash the blueberries. Pour the batter into the prepared pan. Bake at 350° for 50 minutes, or until a toothpick inserted in the center comes out clean. Cool on a rack for 10 minutes.

Makes 1 loaf or 16 slices.

AaBbCcDdEeFfGgHhIiJjKkLlMmNnOoPpQqRrSsTtUuVvWwXxYyZz

When replacing butter with margarine, be sure to choose margarines made with polyunsaturated oils such as canola, corn, and safflower. Find margarines that have liquid oil as their first ingredient.

Corn Bread

This is an all-around favorite. Serve warm with margarine and honey. Corn bread is great with soup or chili.

PAM baking spray
1½ cups cornmeal
½ cup all-purpose flour
1 tablespoon low-sodium baking powder (Featherweight)
½ teaspoon baking soda
1⅛ cups skim milk and 1 tablespoon vinegar (or
   1⅛ cups buttermilk if diet allows)
2 tablespoon frozen unsweetened apple juice
  concentrate
2 egg whites, slightly beaten

Per serving:

98 calories
4% of calories from fat
3.4 gm protein
20.2 gm carbohydrates
0 tsp sugar
0.4 gm fat
69.8 mg sodium
0.4 mg cholesterol

Spray an 8-inch square pan with baking spray. In a medium bowl combine the dry ingredients, mixing well. In a 2-cup measuring cup combine the milk and vinegar. Let the mixture stand for 5 minutes.

In a large bowl combine the curdled milk, apple juice, and egg whites, mixing well with a wire whisk. Add the dry ingredients to the liquid ingredients, blending with a fork just until moistened. Pour the batter into the prepared pan. Bake at 400° for 20 minutes. Cool in the pan on a wire rack.

Serves 12.

Q

Are people who take vitamin supplements better off nutritionally than those who don't?

Studies show that eating a balanced diet provides all of the vitamins and minerals that you need. There are exceptions, and you should consult with a doctor before taking any supplements or giving them to children.

Cranberry Bread

I make this bread for holiday gifts and serve it at our house on Christmas morning.

PAM baking spray
1 cup all-purpose flour
1 cup whole-wheat flour
½ cup sugar
2 tablespoons low-sodium baking powder
   (Featherweight)
½ teaspoon baking soda
2 tablespoons corn oil
4 teaspoons grated orange peel
¾ cup freshly squeezed orange juice
2 egg whites
1¼ cups fresh cranberries,
   chopped in a food processor
¼ cup chopped pecans

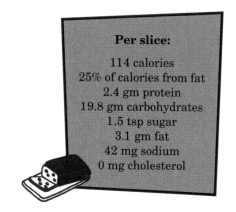

Per slice:

114 calories
25% of calories from fat
2.4 gm protein
19.8 gm carbohydrates
1.5 tsp sugar
3.1 gm fat
42 mg sodium
0 mg cholesterol

Spray a 9 x 5-inch loaf pan with baking spray. In a large bowl combine the dry ingredients, mixing well. In a small bowl combine the oil, orange peel, orange juice, and egg whites, mixing well with a wire whisk. Add the liquid ingredients to the dry ingredients, stirring with a fork just until moistened. Fold in the cranberries and pecans. Pour the batter into the prepared pan. Bake at 350° for 50 minutes to 1 hour. Cool on a wire rack for 15 minutes, then remove from the pan.

   Best when served the next day. Refrigerate overnight in a plastic bag.
   Makes 1 loaf or 16 slices.

Irish Soda Bread

Perfect for Saint Patrick's Day!

PAM baking spray
3 cups all-purpose flour
½ cup sugar
1½ tablespoons low-sodium baking powder
   (Featherweight)
1 teaspoon baking soda
¼ cup Promise margarine, softened
2 egg whites, lightly beaten
1⅛ cups skim milk and 1 tablespoon vinegar
   (or 1⅛ cups buttermilk if diet allows)
2 tablespoons caraway seeds
1 cup raisins
1 teaspoon nutmeg

Per slice:
222 calories
16% of calories from fat
4.9 gm protein
42.7 gm carbohydrates
2 tsp sugar
3.9 gm fat
117.8 mg sodium
0.4 mg cholesterol

Spray a 9-inch round cake pan with baking spray. In a large bowl combine the flour, sugar, baking powder, and baking soda. Cut in the margarine with a fork. If you wish, you may use your hands. In a 2-cup measuring cup combine the egg whites and curdled milk. Stir quickly into the flour mixture. Add the remaining ingredients. Turn the dough onto a well-floured surface. Knead lightly. Shape into an 8-inch circle and place in the prepared cake pan. With a floured knife, make crosswise and lengthwise cuts almost through the dough. Bake at 375° for 35 to 40 minutes.

Makes 1 loaf or 12 slices.

Q To get your daily quota of fiber, you need to eat more of which food: French bread, long-grain rice, or kidney beans?

Kidney beans. A ½-cup serving of cooked dried kidney beans has 4 grams of fiber. Most of us eat less than half of the recommended 20 to 30 grams of fiber daily.

Bunny Buns

These buns are an Easter favorite at our house.

4½ to 5 cups all-purpose flour
2 packages Fleischmann's RapidRise Yeast
¼ teaspoon salt
⅔ cup undiluted evaporated skim milk
½ cup water
½ cup honey
½ cup Promise margarine
4 egg whites, at room temperature
PAM baking spray
½ cup honey
½ cup Promise margarine
45 raisins

> **Per bunny:**
>
> 275 calories
> 30% of calories from fat
> 5.6 gm protein
> 43.2 gm carbohydrates
> 0 tsp sugar
> 9.2 gm fat
> 163.7 mg sodium
> 0.3 mg cholesterol

In a large bowl combine 1½ cups of flour, the yeast, and salt. Set aside. In a medium saucepan heat the milk, water, ½ cup of honey, and ½ cup of margarine until very warm, about 120° to 130°. Gradually stir the milk mixture into the flour mixture. Beat with an electric mixer at medium speed for 2 minutes. Add the egg whites and ½ cup of flour. Beat at high speed for 2 minutes, occasionally scraping the sides of the bowl with a spatula. With a spoon, stir in enough of the remaining flour to make a stiff dough. Spray a large bowl with baking spray. Place the dough in the prepared bowl. Cover tightly with plastic wrap and refrigerate for 2 hours.

Spray 2 baking sheets with baking spray. On a lightly floured surface, divide the dough into 15 even pieces. Roll each piece into a 20-inch rope. Divide each rope into 1 12-inch strip, 1 5-inch strip, and 3 1-inch strips. Coil a 12-inch strip into a circle for the body. Coil a 5-inch strip into a circle for the head. From the 1-inch pieces form 2 ears and a cottontail. Repeat with the remaining strips. Place the bunnies on the prepared baking sheets. Cover with a clean dish towel and let rise until doubled in size, about 20 minutes.

Bake the bunnies at 375° for 12 to 15 minutes or until golden brown. While the bunnies cook, make the honey glaze. In a small saucepan over medium heat stir together the remaining honey and margarine until the margarine is melted.

When the bunnies are golden brown, remove them to wire racks to cool. While still warm, brush each with honey glaze and add raisins for their eyes and noses. Brush the rolls with glaze again before serving, if desired.

Makes 15 bunnies.

Appetizers and Lunches

Salsa Dip

We enjoy this dip at lunch with corn chips and our favorite sandwiches.

1 16-ounce can no-salt-added whole
  tomatoes, chopped
6 black olives, finely diced
2 tablespoons diced green chilies
2 green onions, thinly sliced
2 teaspoons olive oil
¼ teaspoon garlic powder
1½ teaspoons white wine vinegar
Dash Tabasco sauce

> **Per serving:**
>
> 47 calories
> 45% of calories from fat
> 1.5 gm protein
> 6.4 gm carbohydrates
> 0 tsp sugar
> 2.4 gm fat
> 23.7 mg sodium
> 0 mg cholesterol

In a 2-pint container with an airtight lid, combine all
of the ingredients. Refrigerate for 4 hours to allow the flavors to blend.
  Serves 6.

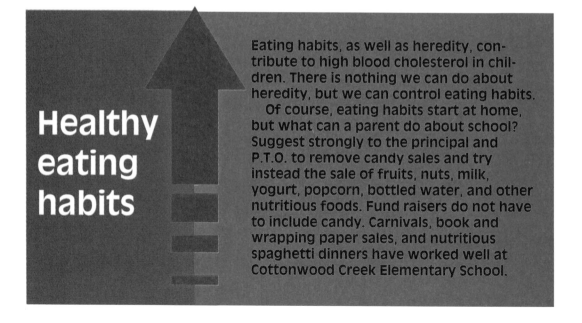

Healthy eating habits

Eating habits, as well as heredity, contribute to high blood cholesterol in children. There is nothing we can do about heredity, but we can control eating habits.
  Of course, eating habits start at home, but what can a parent do about school? Suggest strongly to the principal and P.T.O. to remove candy sales and try instead the sale of fruits, nuts, milk, yogurt, popcorn, bottled water, and other nutritious foods. Fund raisers do not have to include candy. Carnivals, book and wrapping paper sales, and nutritious spaghetti dinners have worked well at Cottonwood Creek Elementary School.

Red Bean Smash

Serve with rice for a great, fast lunch.

1 tablespoon corn oil
3 tablespoons chopped onion
2 cups cooked red kidney beans, drained and puréed
½ cup corn
2 teaspoons no-salt-added tomato paste
2 tablespoons water

Per serving:

152 calories
23% of calories from fat
7.6 gm protein
22.6 gm carbohydrates
0 tsp sugar
3.9 gm fat
5.6 mg sodium
0 mg cholesterol

In a small pan heat the oil and sauté the onion until tender. Add the puréed beans and corn. Stir together the tomato paste and water, and add to the bean mixture. Mix well and heat thoroughly.

Serves 4.

Yogurt Cheese

4 layers cheesecloth
Strainer or small-holed colander
1 16-ounce carton plain nonfat yogurt

Place the cheesecloth over the strainer. Spoon the yogurt into the cheesecloth. Place the strainer over a medium bowl. The liquid from the yogurt will soak through the cheesecloth into the bowl. Cover with plastic wrap and place on a plate. Refrigerate for 12 hours.

Remove from the refrigerator. Spoon the yogurt into a bowl and discard the liquid and cheesecloth. Cover and refrigerate the cheese until ready to use.

Serves 4.

Per serving:

55 calories
0% of calories from fat
6.0 gm protein
7.5 gm carbohydrates
0 tsp sugar
0 gm fat
70.0 mg sodium
0 mg cholesterol

Cheese Spread

This spread is for fruit, nut, or rye bread. Different fruits can be substituted—apples, apricots, and peaches work well.

1 cup low-fat cottage cheese
½ cup crushed pineapple

Blend the 2 ingredients.
Serves 4.

Per serving:

51 calories
12% of calories from fat
7.1 gm protein
3.9 gm carbohydrates
0 tsp sugar
0.7 gm fat
229.8 mg sodium
2.5 mg cholesterol

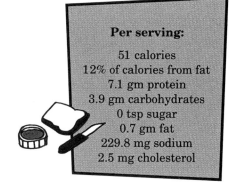

Henny's Salad

Try reading "Chicken Little" to the children while feasting. They love it.

1 cup grated carrots
3 ounces cooked chicken, chopped
¼ cup chopped celery
¼ cup cholesterol-free nonfat mayonnaise
1 tablespoon raisins
Lettuce leaves

Blend together all of the ingredients. Place each serving on a lettuce leaf.
    Serves 4.

Per serving:

74 calories
11% of calories from fat
6.6 gm protein
10 gm carbohydrates
0 tsp sugar
0.9 gm fat
245 mg sodium
16.5 mg cholesterol

Pet Salad (Potatoes, Eggs, and Tuna)

1 tablespoon olive oil
1 teaspoon vinegar
2 boiled potatoes, chopped
4 hard-boiled eggs, yolks discarded and whites chopped
1 6-ounce can low-sodium water-packed tuna, drained
Pepper to taste

In a very small bowl combine the olive oil and vinegar. In a salad bowl combine the remaining ingredients. Add the oil mixture, tossing well.
    Serves 4.

Per serving:

132 calories
25% of calories from fat
14.5 gm protein
9.6 gm carbohydrates
0 tsp sugar
3.7 gm fat
65.6 mg sodium
22.5 mg cholesterol

Tuna Bake

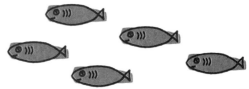

This dish is a little different, but worth a try.

2 egg whites, beaten
¼ cup skim milk
1 tablespoon corn oil
2 tablespoons chopped onion
1 tablespoon parsley
½ teaspoon basil
1 6-ounce can low-sodium water-packed tuna, drained
1 cucumber, grated
¼ cup cholesterol-free nonfat mayonnaise
¼ cup plain nonfat yogurt
1 tablespoon lemon juice
1 teaspoon parsley
½ teaspoon paprika

Per serving:

105 calories
32% of calories from fat
13 gm protein
3.6 gm carbohydrates
0 tsp sugar
3.7 gm fat
71 mg sodium
23.1 mg cholesterol

In a medium bowl combine the egg whites, milk, oil, onion, parsley, and basil. Add the flaked tuna. Pour the mixture into a small ovenproof casserole. Bake at 400° for 25 minutes.

In a small bowl combine the remaining ingredients. Pour the sauce over the cooked casserole.

Serves 4.

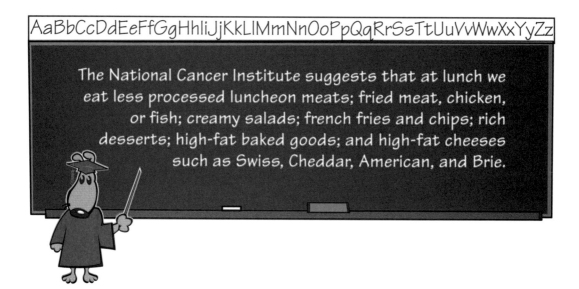

AaBbCcDdEeFfGgHhIiJjKkLlMmNnOoPpQqRrSsTtUuVvWwXxYyZz

The National Cancer Institute suggests that at lunch we eat less processed luncheon meats; fried meat, chicken, or fish; creamy salads; french fries and chips; rich desserts; high-fat baked goods; and high-fat cheeses such as Swiss, Cheddar, American, and Brie.

Peanut Butter Spread

Good old peanut butter with a slightly different twist.

½ cup creamy peanut butter
⅓ cup grated carrots
¼ cup plain nonfat yogurt
1 to 2 tablespoons honey
8 slices whole-wheat bread

In a medium bowl combine the first 4 ingredients until well blended. Spread 4 slices of bread with the spread, then top with the remaining slices of bread.

　Makes 4 sandwiches.

Per sandwich:

313 calories
46% of calories from fat
13.9 gm protein
33.4 gm carbohydrates
0.1 tsp sugar
16.2 gm fat
438.4 mg sodium
2.3 mg cholesterol

Instead of:	Try these:
• Chinese deep fried sweet and sour dishes, fried rice, lemon chicken	• steamed dumplings, soups, lo mein, stir-fry dishes
• Deli sandwiches with bologna, salami, or liverwurst, or salads with mayonnaise	• lean ham, turkey breast, or bar-becued chicken, bean or veg-etable salads
• Italian sausage dishes, fried fish, breaded chicken or veal, buttery or cheesy sauces	• ricotta-filled pasta, plain red sauces, seafood marinara
• Mexican tacos, sour cream, fried foods	• tortillas, fajitas
• Pizzas with sausage or pepperoni	• vegetable toppings

Cream Cheese and Cucumber Sandwich

6 ounces Kraft Philadelphia Free Cream Cheese
2 tablespoons nonfat plain yogurt
½ teaspoon dill weed
Pepper to taste
8 slices bread
16 thin slices cucumber
4 tablespoons alfalfa sprouts
1 tablespoon unsalted sunflower seeds
Lemon

Per sandwich:

175 calories
14% of calories from fat
12 gm protein
25.2 gm carbohydrates
0.1 tsp sugar
2.8 gm fat
503.2 mg sodium
9.7 mg cholesterol

In a small bowl combine the first 4 ingredients. Spread the mixture on 4 slices of bread. Arrange 4 slices of cucumber over the spread on each of the 4 slices. Top each evenly with alfalfa sprouts and sunflower seeds. Sprinkle lightly with lemon juice. Top each with another slice of bread. Cut each sandwich into four pieces for fun, if desired.

Makes 4 sandwiches.

To add variety to sack lunches, you can find alternatives to a sandwich:

- Baked chicken, turkey slices, soup or broth in a thermos, and low-fat fruit yogurt are all excellent accompanied by a slice of whole-wheat bread.

- Try fresh vegetables such as broccoli or cauliflower flowerettes and carrot or celery sticks with a small container of nonfat plain yogurt for dipping.

- Include fresh fruits such as grapes, peaches, pears, plums, bananas, melon wedges, apples, tangerines, oranges, and pineapple wedges. Raisins and dried fruits are great choices as well.

- If milk or juice will not be available at the lunchroom, pack skim milk in a thermos or freeze 100% fruit juice in juice boxes. This will begin to melt by lunch time but will help keep the lunch cool.

Tuna Melt Sandwich

This is great for lunch or dinner. It is an easy Friday night meal.

2 hard-boiled eggs, yolks discarded and whites grated
1 6-ounce can low-sodium water-packed tuna, drained
½ cup finely chopped celery
1 tablespoon minced onion
¼ cup cholesterol-free nonfat mayonnaise
½ teaspoon dill weed
⅛ teaspoon pepper
8 slices whole-wheat bread
½ cup shredded low-fat mild cheddar cheese
4 slices tomato
4 lettuce leaves

Per sandwich:

241 calories
29% of calories from fat
19 gm protein
26 gm carbohydrates
0.1 tsp sugar
7.9 gm fat
416.8 mg sodium
32 mg cholesterol

In a medium bowl combine the first 7 ingredients and stir well. Spread ½ cup of the mixture on each of 4 slices of bread. Top each with 2 tablespoons of cheese. Place the 4 open-faced sandwiches on a baking sheet. Broil 6 inches away from the heat until the cheese melts. Remove from the oven and top each with a tomato slice, a lettuce leaf, and a slice of bread.

   Makes 4 sandwiches.

Expand side-dish horizons

Your child's health doesn't depend on a single food or a single meal, rather on making good nutritional choices over a period of time. Usually there are nutritional equivalents that can be substituted for the foods your child refuses to eat.
   Encourage your child to try three different foods at each meal, but don't be locked into thinking that these must be traditional mealtime foods. Apple wedges, Veggie Muffins (page 56), or Peanut Butter Spread (page 69) on whole-wheat bread can make a good side dish in place of a traditional vegetable.

Veggie Sandwich

This is my favorite sandwich. It is good as an evening meal, too.

2 tablespoons cholesterol-free nonfat mayonnaise
2 teaspoons low-sodium soy sauce
8 slices pumpernickel bread
½ cup shredded carrots
1 cup shredded lettuce
¼ cup unsalted sunflower seeds
½ cup alfalfa sprouts
5 black olives, chopped
4 tomato slices
16 thin zucchini slices
4 thin slices of white onion

Per sandwich:

247 calories
23% of calories from fat
8.9 gm protein
42.9 gm carbohydrates
0.3 tsp sugar
6.2 gm fat
597.9 mg sodium
0 mg cholesterol

In a small bowl combine the mayonnaise and soy sauce. Spread the mixture on 4 slices of bread. Place ¼ of each of the remaining ingredients over the mayonnaise mixture on each slice of bread. Top with the remaining bread and serve.

Makes 4 sandwiches.

Some fun lunch box ideas:

• *Use cookie cutters to make sandwiches in the shapes of animals or toys.*

• *Shape foods in unusual ways, such as ham or turkey roll-ups, or for older children use toothpicks to hold cut vegetables in the shape of boats or buildings.*

• *Draw faces on bananas, oranges, or tangerines (fruits with discardable peels).*

• *Include jokes or messages written on paper napkins, or funny pictures cut from magazines and newspapes.*

• *If you use paper bags, decorate them with markers, stickers, or crayons. You can use stickers to close folding-type sandwich bags, as well.*

Dinners

Ground Beef and Linguine

8 ounces egg-free linguine
1 teaspoon olive oil
½ pound very lean ground beef
1 pound zucchini, sliced
1 16-ounce can no-salt-added whole peeled tomatoes,
  chopped and liquid reserved
1 tablespoon basil
½ teaspoon oregano
⅛ teaspoon thyme
Dash garlic powder
Pepper to taste
Parmesan cheese

Per serving:

102 calories
32% of calories from fat
10 gm protein
7.8 gm carbohydrate
0 tsp sugar
3.6 gm fat
25.8 mg sodium
22 mg cholesterol

Cook the pasta without salt or oil according to the package directions. Drain.

In a wok heat the olive oil over medium high heat. Brown the meat in the oil. Add the zucchini, stir-frying for 1 minute. Add the reserved tomato juice and remaining ingredients except the linguine and Parmesan cheese. Bring to a boil, reduce the heat, and simmer for 4 to 5 minutes. Add the cooked linguine and mix well. Heat through.

Top each serving with Parmesan cheese.

Serves 6.

Put meals in a new perspective

Schedule meals for times when everyone can be there. If evening activities get in the way too often, consider cutting back on outside family commitments. Or perhaps make a house rule that everyone must be home for dinner on certain nights of the week.

Make conversation, not eating, the focus of the meal. Discuss the day's events, current world events, plans for the weekend, or books and articles read recently.

Eggplant Pasta

The leftovers are great as a cold pasta salad.

12 ounces uncooked angel hair pasta
1 medium eggplant (16 ounces)
1 tablespoon olive oil
1 tablespoon red wine vinegar
3 green onions, white parts thinly sliced
¼ teaspoon minced garlic
¼ teaspoon crushed red pepper flakes
Dash pepper
1 16-ounce can no-salt-added tomatoes, chopped
1 teaspoon parsley

Per serving:

197 calories
14% of calories from fat
6.41 gm protein
37.1 gm carbohydrates
0 tsp sugar
3.2 gm fat
5.3 mg sodium
0 mg cholesterol

Cook the pasta without salt or oil according to the package directions. Drain.

Trim the ends off the eggplant. Cut the eggplant into ¼-inch slices, then cube. Steam the eggplant for 10 minutes. Transfer to a large bowl.

In a measuring cup combine the oil, vinegar, onions, garlic, pepper flakes, and pepper. Add this mixture to the eggplant and toss. Stir in the tomatoes, pasta, and parsley.

Serve warm or at room temperature.

Serves 6.

Make dinner cheerful

Children who have positive experiences during family meals are more likely to develop healthy attitudes toward food. This is an opportunity to reinforce good eating habits and introduce a wider variety of foods. Recent research shows that parents and children who eat meals together regularly are more emotionally healthy than those who do not.

Chicken Ties

6 ounces bow tie pasta or any shape pasta
   (about 2 cups uncooked)
2 14½-ounce cans no-salt-added stewed tomatoes
½ pound boneless chicken, cut into ½-inch squares
½ cup onion, chopped
2 cups sliced mushrooms
½ clove garlic, minced
½ teaspoon rosemary
¼ cup shredded Parmesan cheese

Per serving:

123 calories
18% of calories from fat
14.3 gm protein
10.6 gm carbohydrates
0 tsp sugar
2.5 gm fat
77.8 mg sodium
31.3 mg cholesterol

Cook the pasta without salt or oil according to the
package directions. Drain.

Drain the liquid from the tomatoes into a large, nonstick skillet. Bring the liquid
to a boil. Add the chicken, onion, mushrooms, and garlic. Sauté, stirring frequently. After 5 minutes, or when the chicken is browned, stir in the tomatoes and rosemary. Continue cooking for 6 to 8 minutes or until the chicken is thoroughly
cooked. Toss in the pasta.

Top each serving with Parmesan cheese.

Serves 6.

Tips for the cook

Instead of banning meat, which is rich in protein,
iron, and zinc, trim the visible fat from all meats
and serve fish and skinless chicken more often
than beef.

To use fresh herbs in a recipe that calls for
dried, triple the amount specified. Herbs and
spices should be kept in a cool, dry place away
from the sun and stove. Herbs and spices keep for
about 6 months. Write the date on the containers
the day of purchase and discard old and weak
herbs and spices.

Beef and Bow Tie Pasta

1 9-ounce lean sirloin steak, partially frozen
2 cups uncooked bow tie pasta
PAM baking spray
2 to 3 tablespoons red wine
1 carrot, sliced into ¼-inch slices
1 stalk celery, sliced into ¼-inch slices
3 green onions, white parts thinly sliced
2 teaspoons thyme
1 teaspoon parsley
¼ teaspoon black pepper
Dash cayenne pepper
1 cup no-salt-added French-style green beans

Per serving:
211 calories
16% of calories from fat
17.6 gm protein
25.3 gm carbohydrates
0 tsp sugar
3.8 gm fat
49.1 mg sodium
39 mg cholesterol

Trim any fat from the steak. Slice the steak diagonally across the grain into ⅛-inch strips. Cut these strips into bite-sized pieces and set aside.

Cook the pasta without salt or oil according to the package directions. Drain, rinse with warm water, and set aside.

Spray a large nonstick skillet with baking spray. Heat the wine in the skillet over medium high heat. Add the steak, carrots, celery, and onions, and sauté for 3 to 5 minutes or until the meat is browned. Add the seasonings, green beans, and pasta. Toss gently and heat through. Serve immediately.

Serves 6.

AaBbCcDdEeFfGgHhIiJjKkLlMmNnOoPpQqRrSsTtUuVvWwXxYyZz

Dry wine makes a very good marinade, since it adds a fine, subtle taste that does not interfere with the flavor of the meat. The acid content of wine helps break down fibers, tenderizing inexpensive, tougher cuts of lean meats. Remember that cooking wines often have a high sodium content, so always check the label.

Mama's Spaghetti Sauce

1 tablespoon olive oil
1 cup diced onion
½ cup chopped celery
1½ cups sliced fresh mushrooms
1 16-ounce can no-salt-added tomatoes, chopped and
  juice reserved
1 8-ounce can no-salt-added tomato paste
8 black olives, sliced
1 bay leaf
Dash garlic powder
1 teaspoon oregano
½ teaspoon basil
¼ cup chopped fresh parsley (or 1 tablespoon dried flakes)
12 ounces spaghetti (angel hair has a great texture)

> **Per serving:**
>
> 177 calories
> 21% of calories from fat
> 6.0 gm protein
> 31.4 gm carbohydrates
> 0 tsp sugar
> 4.1 gm fat
> 69.3 mg sodium
> 0 mg cholesterol

In a nonstick skillet heat the oil over medium high heat and sauté the onion, celery, and mushrooms until softened. Stir in the tomatoes, juice, tomato paste, olives, and seasonings. Cover and cook 30 minutes over low heat. Remove the bay leaf.

Cook the spaghetti without salt or oil according to the package directions. Drain. Divide among 6 plates and top with sauce.

Serves 6.

AaBbCcDdEeFfGgHhIiJjKkLlMmNnOoPpQqRrSsTtUuVvWwXxYyZz

Fats have 9 calories per gram. They provide energy and help the body to use vitamins. Carbohydrates have 4 calories per gram. They provide energy for physical and mental activities. Protein has 4 calories per gram. Proteins build and rebuild the body, and help form a part of every cell in the body.

Meatballs in Tomato Sauce

1 16-ounce can no-salt-added tomato sauce
1 16-ounce can no-salt-added whole tomatoes, chopped
  and liquid reserved
1 tablespoon Italian seasoning
⅛ teaspoon pepper
⅛ teaspoon garlic powder
PAM baking spray
¼ cup finely diced onion
¾ pound very lean ground beef
¼ cup soft bread crumbs
⅛ cup nonfat milk
1 tablespoon dried parsley
½ teaspoon oregano
¼ teaspoon pepper
1 egg white
8 ounces thin egg-free spaghetti

Per serving:

136 calories
9% of calories from fat
8.3 gm protein
22.9 gm carbohydrates
0 tsp sugar
1.4 gm fat
45.7 mg sodium
10.3 mg cholesterol

In a medium saucepan combine the tomato sauce, tomatoes, Italian seasoning, pepper, and garlic powder. Bring the mixture to a boil. Reduce the heat and simmer uncovered for 30 minutes, stirring occasionally. Meanwhile, prepare the meatballs.

Spray a nonstick skillet with baking spray. In the prepared skillet sauté the onions until transparent. Transfer the onions to a large bowl. Add the ground beef, bread crumbs, milk, parsley, oregano, pepper, and egg white, mixing well. (I find that using my hands to mix this works well.) Shape into 20 meatballs about 1 inch in diameter.

Spray a baking sheet with baking spray. Arrange the meatballs on the prepared baking sheet. Bake at 375° for 15 to 18 minutes, or until browned. While the meatballs are baking, prepare the spaghetti.

Cook the spaghetti without salt or oil according to the package directions. Drain. Divide the spaghetti among 4 plates. Top each with the sauce and meatballs.

Serves 6.

Pappy's Pasta

Serve this over orzo, a tiny rice-shaped pasta, or thin spaghetti. The credit for this recipe goes to my husband, Rusty.

½ **pound skinned, boned chicken breasts**
1 **tablespoon olive oil**
½ **large onion, chopped**
¼ **cup chopped green bell pepper (optional)**
½ **clove garlic, minced**
1½ **cups sliced mushrooms**
1 **medium zucchini, sliced**
1 **16-ounce can no-salt-added whole tomatoes, chopped**
1 **teaspoon basil**
½ **teaspoon Italian seasonings**
⅛ **teaspoon Tabasco sauce**
1 **tablespoon cornstarch**

> **Per serving:**
>
> 102 calories
> 32% of calories from fat
> 10 gm protein
> 7.8 gm carbohydrates
> 0 tsp sugar
> 3.6 gm fat
> 25.8 mg sodium
> 22 mg cholesterol

Cut the chicken in ½-inch slices. Heat a wok or nonstick skillet over medium high heat. Add the olive oil and heat. Sauté the chicken, onion, bell pepper, and garlic for 5 minutes, or until the chicken is cooked on the outside.

Stir in the mushrooms and zucchini, and sauté for 2 minutes. Drain the tomatoes, reserving the juice. Add the tomatoes to the wok, along with the seasonings. In a small cup blend together the cornstarch and reserved tomato juice. Pour the mixture over the chicken mixture in the wok. Bring to a boil, stirring constantly, until the liquid thickens.

Serves 6.

Look at the options

Pastas and grains are not highly caloric. It is the creamy or cheesy sauces that add the fat and calories.
If your child does not eat meat, try eggs, poultry, fish, low-fat cheese, beans, peanut butter, or tofu.

Pasta Primavera

1 carrot, peeled and cut into julienne strips
1 small sweet red pepper, seeded and cut into julienne
   strips
1 zucchini squash, cut into julienne strips
⅛ pound stemmed snow peas
6 large ripe plum tomatoes
8 ounces egg-free fettucine
1 teaspoon corn oil
⅛ cup cooking sherry
1 tablespoon olive oil
1 teaspoon dill
½ teaspoon chives
2 green onions, white parts thinly sliced
Parmesan cheese, if desired

Per serving:

241 calories
21% of calories from fat
7.5 gm protein
40.9 gm carbohydrates
0.1 tsp sugar
5.5 gm fat
34.5 mg sodium
0 mg cholesterol

Fill a medium saucepan with water and bring to a boil. Drop in the julienned carrot and red pepper. After 30 seconds, add the julienned zucchini and snow peas. Blanch for another minute, then transfer all of the vegetables with a slotted spoon to a colander. Rinse with cold water, then pat dry with a paper towel. Set aside.

In the same pan of boiling water gently add the tomatoes. Boil for 1 minute, then remove with a long-handled fork. Let the tomatoes cool slightly, then remove their skins. Slice in ½-inch slices. Place the tomato slices in a small saucepan. Set aside.

Cook the fettucine without salt or oil according to the package directions. Drain and rinse with hot water. Transfer to a large bowl and toss gently with the corn oil. Set aside.

To the saucepan containing the tomatoes add the sherry, olive oil, dill, chives, and green onions. Bring to a gentle boil over medium high heat. Reduce the heat to low and simmer for 5 more minutes.

Turn the tomato mixture into the fettucine, tossing lightly. Add the blanched vegetables, tossing again. Serve right away, with Parmesan cheese if desired.

Serves 4.

Spaghetti with Raisins

Quick & Easy

A quick and easy meal. Serve with sourdough or French bread and a green salad.

¼ cup golden raisins
½ cup warm water
¼ cup white wine
¼ cup chopped white onion
1 clove garlic, minced
10 ounces spaghetti
1 16-ounce can no-salt-added tomatoes, chopped
1 8-ounce can no-salt-added tomato paste
8 black olives, sliced
¼ teaspoon black pepper
1 6½-ounce can low-sodium water-packed tuna, drained

Per serving:

274 calories
9% of calories from fat
19.6 gm protein
42.3 gm carbohydrates
0 tsp sugar
2.8 gm fat
90.6 mg sodium
30 mg cholesterol

In a small bowl soak the raisins in ½ cup of warm water.

In a nonstick skillet heat the wine and sauté the onion and garlic until soft, about 10 minutes.

In the meantime, cook the spaghetti without salt or oil according to the package directions. Drain and rinse with cool water. Set aside in a colander.

In the skillet with the onions add the raisins and their water, tomatoes, tomato paste, olives, and pepper. Cook over medium heat for 5 minutes. Add the tuna chunks and warm through. Pour the sauce over the spaghetti and serve.

Serves 4.

Find substitutes for salt

The average person in the United States consumes 10 to 20 times the amount of sodium needed. Small amounts of sodium are used by the body to uphold and regulate the correct water balance. Excess sodium is thought to contribute to water retention, high blood pressure, and kidney disease.

To supply a salty taste, try dehydrated onion flakes or onion powder, lemon juice, garlic flakes or powder, celery seed, parsley, or hot pepper sauce.

Spaghett·i·Roni

A Friday night special at our house. This is a great change from boxed macaroni and cheese. It is nutritionally better than macaroni and cheese, but not a dinner to serve frequently.

PAM baking spray
1 16-ounce jar Newman's Own meatless spaghetti sauce
⅓ cup water
7½ ounces low-fat ricotta cheese
6 egg whites
1 teaspoon oregano
1 cup uncooked Creamettes elbow macaroni
6 ounces skim milk mozzarella cheese, shredded

Per serving:
223 calories
47% of calories from fat
16.4 gm protein
12.7 gm carbohydrates
0 tsp sugar
11.7 gm fat
434.7 mg sodium
28.7 mg cholesterol

Spray a 10 x 7 x 2-inch glass baking dish with baking spray. In a medium bowl combine the spaghetti sauce and water. Set aside.

In a blender combine the ricotta cheese, egg whites, and oregano. Blend well.

Spoon ⅓ of the spaghetti sauce into the prepared baking dish. Scatter ½ cup of macaroni over the sauce. Spread ½ of the ricotta cheese mixture over the macaroni, then top with ⅓ of the shredded mozzarella. Repeat the layers, ending with the tomato sauce. Reserve ⅓ of the mozzarella for later. Cover with aluminum foil.

Bake at 350° for 45 minutes. Remove the foil and sprinkle the remaining mozzarella over the top. Bake an additional 15 minutes. Let the dish stand for 10 minutes before serving.

Serves 6.

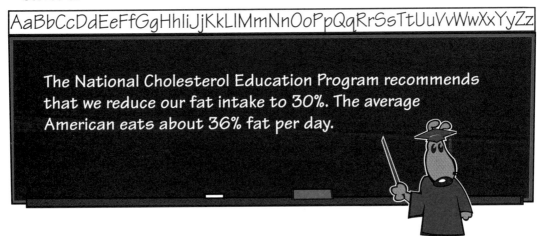

AaBbCcDdEeFfGgHhIiJjKkLlMmNnOoPpQqRrSsTtUuVvWwXxYyZz

The National Cholesterol Education Program recommends that we reduce our fat intake to 30%. The average American eats about 36% fat per day.

Vegetarian Lasagna

Quite a masterpiece. Adult guests appreciate the effort and enjoy the results. Serve with French bread and a crisp green salad.

1 onion, diced
1 clove garlic, minced
1 pound unpeeled eggplant, chopped into 1/2-inch
    squares
6 ounces spinach, cleaned and stemmed
½ pound fresh mushrooms, sliced
1 16-ounce can no-salt-added whole tomatoes, chopped
    and juice reserved
1 8-ounce can no-salt-added tomato paste
1 8-ounce can no-salt-added tomato sauce
¼ cup dry red wine or sherry
2 carrots, shredded
2 teaspoons oregano
1 teaspoon basil
Pepper to taste
1 2¼-ounce can sliced black olives
9 lasagna noodles
16 ounces skim milk ricotta cheese
2 egg whites
PAM baking spray
1 cup grated skim milk mozzarella cheese
Parmesan cheese

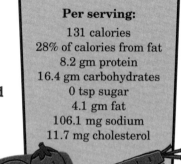

Per serving:
131 calories
28% of calories from fat
8.2 gm protein
16.4 gm carbohydrates
0 tsp sugar
4.1 gm fat
106.1 mg sodium
11.7 mg cholesterol

In a large saucepan over medium heat, cook the onion, garlic, eggplant, spinach, and mushrooms in the reserved tomato juice for 15 minutes. Add the tomatoes, tomato paste, tomato sauce, wine, carrots, oregano, basil, and pepper. Bring to a boil over medium high heat. Lower the heat, cover, and simmer for 30 minutes. Stir occasionally. Add the drained black olives, then set aside.

While the sauce is simmering, cook the lasagna noodles without salt or oil according to the package directions. Drain, and cover the noodles with lukewarm water. Place a piece of waxed paper about 16 inches long on the counter and carefully place the noodles flat on the waxed paper.

In a blender, process the ricotta cheese and egg whites until smooth.

Spray a 9 x 13-inch baking dish with baking spray. Lay 3 noodles lengthwise across the pan. Spread 4 tablespoons of the ricotta mixture on each noodle.

Cover with a layer of the tomato sauce, then sprinkle with ⅓ of the mozzarella cheese. Repeat the layers 2 more times, ending with the mozzarella cheese. Top with the Parmesan cheese.

Bake at 350° for 45 minutes, or until bubbling. Remove the lasagna from the oven and let it rest for 10 minutes.

Serves 12.

Yellow Summer Squash and Linguine

The leftovers make a great cold pasta salad.

2 tablespoons pine nuts
7 medium to large tomatoes, peeled, seeded, and chopped
2 tablespoons chopped walnuts
1 2¼-ounce can sliced black olives (optional)
1 shallot, chopped
½ clove garlic, minced
1 teaspoon basil
1 teaspoon thyme
Pinch red pepper
8 ounces egg-free linguine
1 tablespoon olive oil
2 large yellow summer squashes, sliced in ¼-inch slices

Per serving:
166 calories
32.5% of calories from fat
5.1 gm protein
24.6 gm carbohydrates
0 tsp sugar
6 gm fat
5.6 mg sodium
0 mg cholesterol

On a baking sheet, spread out the pine nuts and bake at 275° for 5 to 7 minutes. Cool.

In a large bowl combine the pine nuts, tomatoes, walnuts, olives, shallot, garlic, basil, thyme, and red pepper. Let the mixture sit on the counter for 1 hour before serving.

Meanwhile, cook the linguine without salt or oil according to the package directions. Drain and rinse. In a nonstick skillet heat the oil and sauté the squash until soft. In a large bowl combine the linguine and the squash, mixing well.

Divide the linguine mixture among 6 plates. Top each serving with tomato sauce.

Refrigerate any leftovers.

Serves 6.

Zucchini, Tomatoes, and Linguine

This goes well with a green salad or Fresh Fruit Salad and sourdough bread. The leftovers are tasty as a cold pasta salad.

PAM baking spray
8 ounces egg-free linguine
1 teaspoon olive oil
½ cup white wine
1 cup chopped white onions
½ green pepper, chopped
1 zucchini, thinly sliced
6 tomatoes, peeled, seeded, and cut into strips
¼ cup Parmesan cheese

Per serving:

159 calories
20% of calories from fat
5.4 gm protein
24.9 gm carbohydrates
0 tsp sugar
3.6 gm fat
54.8 mg sodium
2 mg cholesterol

Spray a 2-quart casserole with baking spray. Cook the linguine without salt or oil according to the package directions. Drain and rinse. Turn the linguine into the prepared casserole and stir in the olive oil.

In a large nonstick skillet over medium high heat, add the wine and sauté the onion for 5 minutes. Add the green pepper and sauté for 2 minutes. Add the zucchini and sauté for 2 more minutes. Remove from the heat and stir in the tomatoes. Stir the vegetable mixture into the noodles. Top with Parmesan cheese. Cover and bake at 350° for 30 minutes.

Serves 6.

Meals can be educational

Once a month pick a country and plan a menu around the popular dishes of that country. Make simple decorations and learn a few words and phrases of the language, such as "hello," "please," and "thank you."

Chicken and Bulgur

This is an easy, quick recipe. Depending on your family, you may have some left-overs for lunch.

3 pounds chicken parts, skinned
1 13¾-ounce can Pritikin chicken broth
1 cup cold water
1 cup bulgur wheat
1 small onion, chopped
½ teaspoon curry
¼ teaspoon garlic, crushed
⅛ teaspoon black pepper
2 cups sliced carrots (about 4)
1 cup sliced zucchini (about 1 medium)
½ cup chopped green pepper (about ½)

Per serving:

282 calories
16% of calories from fat
32.1 gm protein
28.3 gm carbohydrates
0 tsp sugar
4.9 gm fat
127.5 mg sodium
73.4 mg cholesterol

In a Dutch oven combine the first 8 ingredients. Bring the mixture to a boil. Reduce the heat, cover, and simmer for 10 minutes.

Turn the chicken over and add the carrots. Cover and simmer for 15 minutes. Add the zucchini and green pepper. Cover and simmer another 10 minutes or until the chicken is cooked through.

Serves 6.

Fat grams per 5-ounce raw serving of chicken pieces with and without skin:

Piece:	with skin	without skin
breast	13	2
drumstick	12	5
wing	23	5
thigh	22	6

Chicken with Orange Sauce

4 5-ounce chicken breast halves, skinned
1½ cups orange juice
¼ cup dry white wine
2 teaspoons oregano
½ teaspoon thyme
¼ teaspoon ground black pepper
Dash garlic powder
Paprika
1 tablespoon cornstarch
2 tablespoons water
¼ cup orange marmalade
1 cup long-grain white rice, cooked (or Wild Rice
   recipe, p. 130)

Per serving:

235 calories
13% of calories from fat
25.3 gm protein
23 gm carbohydrates
1.3 tsp sugar
3.4 gm fat
57.5 mg sodium
66 mg cholesterol

In a large, microwave-safe glass baking dish, arrange the chicken. In a small bowl combine the orange juice, wine, and seasonings. Pour the sauce over the chicken. Sprinkle with paprika and cover with waxed paper.

Microwave on high for 5 minutes. Turn the chicken breasts over and rotate the dish. Cover and microwave on high for 5 minutes. Turn the dish twice during cooking. Cut into one piece of chicken to the bone to make sure it is not pink. Cook a little longer if necessary.

In a 4-cup glass measure, combine the cornstarch and 2 tablespoons of water. Add the marmalade and the pan juices. Cover with waxed paper and microwave on high for 4 to 5 minutes, until the sauce thickens. Serve the sauce over the chicken and rice.

Serves 4.

Some poultry precautions

Even when the outside of chicken feels frozen, the inside meat may not be. Treat the chicken like any other fresh meat. Refrigerate or freeze the chicken as soon as possible. Use refrigerated chcken within 1 to 2 days. Frozen chicken will keep for about 9 to 12 months. Cook chicken until no pink remains.

Chicken Burritos

½ pound boneless, skinless chicken breasts
6 flour tortillas
1 tablespoon olive oil
1 medium onion, chopped
⅛ cup white wine
1 14½-ounce can no-salt-added Mexican-
   style stewed tomatoes
½ teaspoon oregano
2 teaspoons red wine vinegar

Per serving:

156 calories
26% of calories from fat
13.6 gm protein
14.5 gm carbohydrates
0 tsp sugar
4.5 gm fat
58.4 mg sodium
29.3 mg cholesterol

Microwave the chicken on high for 5 minutes or until no longer pink inside. Cut the chicken into bite-sized pieces.

Wrap the tortillas and heat in a warm oven for 10 minutes to soften.

In a medium nonstick skillet heat the oil over medium high heat. Add the onions and sauté for 5 minutes. Add a little wine as needed to prevent sticking. Drain the tomato liquid into the pan and add the oregano. Increase the heat to high and cook for 3 minutes, stirring frequently. While the vegetable mixture is cooking, chop the tomatoes and place in a small bowl. Add the vinegar and stir. Set aside.

Remove the skillet from the heat. Add the chicken, mixing well. Evenly divide the chicken mixture among the tortillas. Roll up the tortillas and place in a baking dish. Pour the tomato mixture over the burritos. Cover with foil. Bake at 350° for 10 minutes.

Serves 6.

AaBbCcDdEeFfGgHhIiJjKkLlMmNnOoPpQqRrSsTtUuVvWwXxYyZz

Oregano is a member of the mint family and also is known as wild marjoram. It is frequently used in Italian dishes, including pizza, spaghetti, and various tomato sauces. A more pungent Mexican oregano is used in fish and pork dishes, as well as in soups and tomato sauces.

Chicken Enchilada Casserole

¾ pound boneless chicken breasts, skinned
1½ cups sliced fresh mushrooms
1 medium onion, chopped
½ cup chopped green bell pepper
¼ cup nonfat powdered milk
2 tablespoons all-purpose flour
1 cup water
1 teaspoon chili powder
½ teaspoon cumin
½ teaspoon Mrs. Dash
PAM baking spray
4 corn tortillas, halved
¾ cup shredded low-fat, low-sodium cheddar cheese
1 tomato, diced
¼ cup plain nonfat yogurt

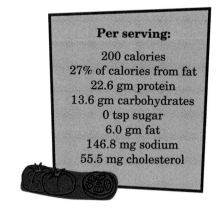

Per serving:

200 calories
27% of calories from fat
22.6 gm protein
13.6 gm carbohydrates
0 tsp sugar
6.0 gm fat
146.8 mg sodium
55.5 mg cholesterol

Microwave the chicken on high for 5 to 7 minutes or until cooked. Set aside to cool.

Spray a large nonstick skillet with baking spray. Over medium high heat sauté the mushrooms, onion, and pepper until the onion is transparent. Cut the cooled chicken into bite-sized pieces. Add the chicken to the vegetable mixture and set aside.

In a small saucepan combine the powdered milk and flour. Slowly stir in the water. Cook over medium heat until thickened, stirring constantly. This takes about 20 minutes.

When thickened, add the white sauce to the chicken mixture. Stir in the seasonings and mix well.

Spray a 2-quart baking dish with baking spray. Place 3 tortilla halves on the bottom. Spoon in ⅓ of the chicken mixture. Repeat the layers, ending with the chicken mixture. Cover with aluminum foil. Bake at 350° for 30 minutes. Uncover and sprinkle with cheese. Heat for another 5 minutes, or until the cheese melts.

Serve topped with tomatoes and a dollop of yogurt.

Serves 6.

Lemon Chicken

PAM baking spray
1 20-ounce package "pick of the chick" combo
   (3 backs, legs, breasts)
1 tablespoon corn oil
3 to 4 tablespoons fresh lemon juice
1 clove garlic, minced
1 teaspoon Mrs. Dash

Per serving:

172 calories
31% of calories from fat
27.3 gm protein
0.6 gm carbohydrates
0 tsp sugar
5.9 gm fat
62 mg sodium
73.3 mg cholesterol

Spray a large baking dish with baking spray. Remove the skin from the chicken. Arrange the chicken in the baking dish. In a small bowl combine the remaining ingredients. Pour the mixture over the chicken. Cover tightly with aluminum foil. Bake at 350° for 40 to 45 minutes, basting every 15 minutes. Uncover and brown for 10 minutes. Do not overcook!
   Serves 6.

To minimize the fat in foods, try these cooking methods:

• Sauté foods in a little broth instead of butter or oil.

• Marinate meats for several hours, and then broil them.

• Stir-fry with nonstick cooking spray or just a teaspoon of oil.

• Steam vegetables to retain color, flavor, and nutrients.

• Roast meats on a rack so the fat will drip away.

• Poach fish or chicken in water, low-sodium broth, or tomato juice.

Limey Chicken

PAM baking spray
3 whole chicken breasts (15 ounces)
¼ teaspoon garlic powder
½ teaspoon Mrs. Dash
1 20-ounce can pineapple slices, drained and liquid
  reserved
¼ cup honey
3 tablespoons pineapple juice
2 tablespoons low-sodium soy sauce
2 tablespoons fresh lime juice (1 lime)
2 teaspoons cornstarch
Grated peel of 1 lime

Per serving:

256 calories
16% of calories from fat
31 gm protein
23.4 gm carbohydrates
0 tsp sugar
4.4 gm fat
68.4 mg sodium
82.5 mg cholesterol

Spray a baking dish with baking spray. Remove the skin from the chicken breasts. This is easiest when still partially frozen. Arrange the chicken in the prepared dish and season on both sides with garlic powder and Mrs. Dash. Bake at 350° for 35 to 45 minutes, or until done.

About 10 minutes before serving, prepare the sauce. In a small saucepan combine the liquid ingredients and cornstarch. Cook over medium heat, stirring with a wire whisk until thickened. Add the pineapple and lime peel. Serve the sauce over the chicken.

Serves 4.

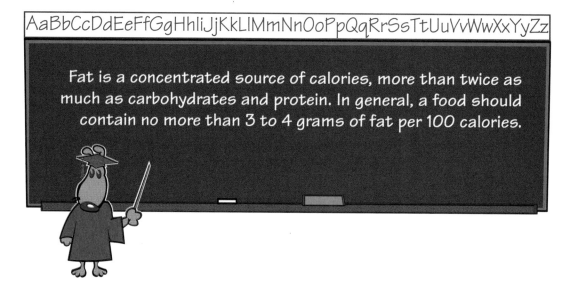

AaBbCcDdEeFfGgHhIiJjKkLlMmNnOoPpQqRrSsTtUuVvWwXxYyZz

Fat is a concentrated source of calories, more than twice as much as carbohydrates and protein. In general, a food should contain no more than 3 to 4 grams of fat per 100 calories.

Paella

Serve with a green salad and orange slices.

¼ cup Pritikin chicken broth
1 cup brown rice
3 green onions
1 clove garlic, minced
1 8-ounce can no-salt-added tomato sauce
1 13¾-ounce can Pritikin chicken broth
1 tablespoon low-sodium soy sauce
1 stalk celery with leaves, diced
2 carrots, peeled and sliced
¼ teaspoon crushed red pepper
1 teaspoon Mrs. Dash
1 bay leaf
½ green pepper, diced
1 cup fresh mushrooms, sliced
1 cup diced cooked chicken breast
4 ounces frozen artichoke hearts
1 cup frozen peas
⅛ teaspoon saffron

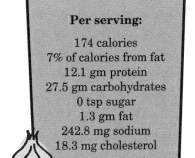

Per serving:

174 calories
7% of calories from fat
12.1 gm protein
27.5 gm carbohydrates
0 tsp sugar
1.3 gm fat
242.8 mg sodium
18.3 mg cholesterol

In a large Dutch oven combine the first 4 ingredients. Cook over medium high heat, stirring constantly, until the rice begins to brown lightly. Stir in the next 8 ingredients and bring to a boil. Reduce the heat, cover, and simmer for 40 minutes.

Stir in the remaining ingredients. Cover and bake at 350° for 20 minutes. Remove the bay leaf before serving.

Serves 6.

Peachy Chicken

Quick & Easy

A green salad completes this meal.

1 16-ounce can unsweetened peach slices
8 ounces boneless, skinless chicken breasts, cut into bite-sized pieces
¼ to ½ cup white wine
½ medium onion, chopped
½ cup red pepper, chopped
1 cup long-grain white rice
½ cup water
1 teaspoon olive oil
½ teaspoon Mrs. Dash
½ clove garlic, minced
1 10-ounce package frozen artichoke hearts

Per serving:
171 calories
13% of calories from fat
14 gm protein
24.8 gm carbohydrates
0 tsp sugar
2.4 gm fat
49 mg sodium
29.3 mg cholesterol

Drain the peaches, reserving the liquid.

In a large nonstick skillet bring the wine to a boil. Add the chicken and brown over high heat. Stir in the onion and pepper and cook for 2 to 3 minutes. Add the reserved peach liquid, rice, water, oil, and seasonings, and bring to a boil. Cover, reduce the heat to medium low, and simmer for 20 to 25 minutes or until the rice is cooked.

Stir in the artichoke hearts and peaches. Heat through and serve.

Serves 6.

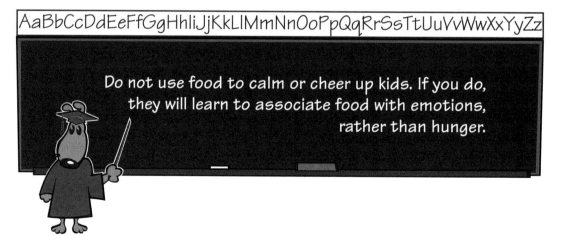

AaBbCcDdEeFfGgHhIiJjKkLlMmNnOoPpQqRrSsTtUuVvWwXxYyZz

Do not use food to calm or cheer up kids. If you do, they will learn to associate food with emotions, rather than hunger.

Potato and Chicken Stir-Fry

1 pound potatoes, peeled and cut into 2-inch
  julienne strips
1 cup rice
2 tablespoons low-sodium soy sauce
½ teaspoon ground ginger
1 tablespoon brown sugar
1 tablespoon orange juice
½ cup Pritikin chicken broth
8 ounces boneless, skinless chicken breasts, cut into
  bite-sized pieces
1 teaspoon sesame oil
Additional chicken broth as needed
½ medium red bell pepper, seeded and thinly sliced
3 green onions, white parts diagonally sliced
4 ounces mushrooms (or bean sprouts)
4 ounces snow peas, rinsed and trimmed

Per serving:

236 calories
14% of calories from fat
22.2 gm protein
29.0 gm carbohydrates
0.8 tsp sugar
3.7 gm fat
394.4 mg sodium
44 mg cholesterol

In a large bowl soak the potato strips in cold water. Cook the rice according to the package directions.

Drain the potatoes and place in a microwave-safe dish. Cover. Microwave on high for 5 minutes, stirring and turning every 1½ minutes.

In a small bowl combine the soy sauce, ginger, brown sugar, and orange juice. Set aside.

While the potatoes and rice are cooking, heat the chicken broth in a wok or non-stick skillet over medium high heat. Add the chicken and cook for 4 to 5 minutes until cooked through. Remove the chicken from the pan with a slotted spoon. Discard the broth.

In a wok heat the oil over medium high heat. Add the potatoes and stir-fry for 2 minutes. Add a little chicken broth as necessary. Add the pepper, onions, and mushrooms and stir-fry for 2 minutes. Add a little chicken broth as necessary to keep the vegetables from sticking. Add the chicken, snow peas, and sauce, stir-frying an additional 2 minutes. Serve over rice.

Serves 4.

Sweet and Sour Chicken

This is good with rice. It is a meal in itself, or you can serve a green salad to complement.

1 20-ounce can unsweetened pineapple chunks, drained
  and juice reserved
3 tablespoons white wine vinegar (or white rice vinegar)
1 tablespoon low-sodium soy sauce
½ teaspoon dry mustard
½ teaspoon Mrs. Dash
2 drops Tabasco sauce
1 1½-pound fryer, cut up and skinned (or 4 breasts)
½ green bell pepper, diced

Per serving:

171 calories
20% of calories from fat
27.5 gm protein
5.1 gm carbohydrates
0 tsp sugar
3.8 gm fat
570.5 mg sodium
73.3 mg cholesterol

In a medium bowl combine the pineapple juice, vinegar, soy sauce, dry mustard, Mrs. Dash, and Tabasco. Mix well.

In a shallow glass baking pan arrange the chicken. Pour the sauce over the chicken. Top with pineapple. Cover with plastic wrap and refrigerator for 1 hour.

Bake at 350° for 40 minutes, basting often. Top the chicken with green pepper and cook another 10 minutes, or until the chicken is done.

Serves 6.

Homemade Tortillas

1 cup all-purpose flour
½ teaspoon salt substitute
1 teaspoon low-sodium baking powder
1 tablespoon corn oil
⅛ cup skim milk, warmed

Per tortilla:

96 calories
23% of calories from fat
2.5 gm protein
15.5 gm carbohydrates
0 tsp sugar
2.5 gm fat
7.3 mg sodium
0.2 mg cholesterol

In a medium bowl combine the flour, salt substitute, and baking powder. Add the oil and stir until well mixed. Add the warmed milk, stirring until a ball is formed. Knead for 5 minutes. Let the dough rest for 20 minutes.

Shape the dough into 6 balls. Roll each ball out

between 2 sheets of waxed paper into a circle ⅛-inch thick. In a nonstick skillet over medium high heat, cook the tortillas until lightly browned in places. Transfer to paper towels, and cover with additional paper towels.

Tostadas

This meal takes about an hour to prepare, but it is one of our favorites. Instead of assembling the tostadas ahead, I allow the children to make their own. I spread the beans, and they do the rest. They love to use the lazy Susan for the ingredients; we just put it on the table and let the tostadas roll.

2 tablespoons olive oil
¼ cup chopped onion
1 16-ounce can whole peeled no-salt-added tomatoes,
    drained and diced
2 tablespoons canned green chilies, chopped
1 teaspoon cilantro
2 cups Rosaritas Vegetarian Refried Beans
8 tortillas (or see Homemade Tortillas recipe, p. 96)
1½ cups grated low-sodium, low-fat cheddar cheese
10 ounces shredded or diced cooked chicken
2½ cups shredded iceberg lettuce
1 ripe avocado, peeled and diced

Per tostada:

408 calories
34% of calories from fat
28.7 gm protein
39.8 gm carbohydrates
0 tsp sugar
15.6 gm fat
190.4 mg sodium
50.2 mg cholesterol

In a skillet heat the olive oil. Sauté the onion until clear. Add the tomatoes, chilies, and cilantro. Simmer for 10 minutes or until slightly thickened. Set aside to cool.

In a small saucepan warm the refried beans over low heat. Place the cheese, chicken, lettuce, and avocado into individual serving bowls.

Spread the warmed refried beans onto the tortillas. Sprinkle each with chicken, lettuce, and cheese. Top each tostada with avocado and the tomato sauce.

Serves 8.

Turkey Chili

We enjoy the chili with a tossed green salad, corn bread, and Brown Pineapple.

1 green pepper, chopped
1 yellow pepper, chopped
½ cup diced onion
1 clove garlic, minced
½ pound ground turkey
1 16-ounce can no-salt-added tomatoes
1 8-ounce can no-salt-added tomato sauce
1 15-ounce can no-salt-added kidney beans,
   rinsed and drained
½ cup raisins
1 tablespoon chili powder
2 teaspoons cilantro
¼ teaspoon ground cloves
¼ teaspoon ground cumin
¼ teaspoon oregano
Salsa (optional)

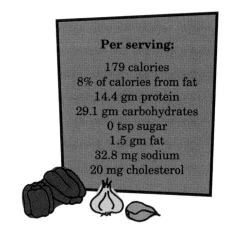

Per serving:

179 calories
8% of calories from fat
14.4 gm protein
29.1 gm carbohydrates
0 tsp sugar
1.5 gm fat
32.8 mg sodium
20 mg cholesterol

In a 3-quart microwave-safe casserole combine the peppers, onion, garlic, and turkey. Cover and microwave on high for 7 to 8 minutes, stirring 4 times, until the turkey is cooked. Drain off the fat and liquid.

Place the casserole on the stove or pour the turkey mixture into a large saucepan, and add the remaining ingredients. Bring to a boil over medium high heat. Reduce the heat and simmer for 15 minutes.

Serve in a bowl. Adults can add salsa for a spicier flavor, if desired.

Serves 6.

Turkey Picadillo

½ pound ground turkey
½ cup chopped onion
½ cup chopped green pepper
¼ cup chopped red pepper
Dash garlic powder
½ teaspoon cinnamon
½ teaspoon ground cumin
¼ teaspoon ground cloves
2 14½-ounce cans no-salt-added stewed tomatoes
1 Granny Smith apple, cored and chopped
¼ cup raisins
2 cups white rice or orzo, cooked

Per serving:

198 calories
11% of calories from fat
20.3 gm protein
25.6 gm carbohydrates
0 tsp sugar
2.4 gm fat
49.6 mg sodium
40 mg cholesterol

In a large nonstick skillet over medium high heat brown the turkey, onion, peppers, and garlic powder. Sauté until the turkey is no longer pink. Drain.

Stir in the next 6 ingredients. Bring the picadillo to a boil. Reduce the heat, cover, and simmer for 25 minutes.

Serve over rice or orzo.

Serves 4.

Add some magic to family mealtimes

- It is fun to throw a spontaneous party. Consider celebrating such things as the arrival of an out-of-town guest, the first snow, the family pet's birthday or anniversary with your family, the last day of exams, and the special achievements of family members.

- Occasionally ask a family member to contribute a poem, interesting article, story, or show a new award or gift to the family.

- Make dinners special. Try new ways to fold napkins, light candles, vary the centerpice, or occasionaly make place cards.

- Let children pick out their own inexpensive dinner plates and silverware, even for everyday use. Just make sure it's washable and not fragile.

Turkey Pie

PAM baking spray
1 pound ground turkey
½ clove garlic, minced
½ medium onion, chopped
½ cup green pepper, seeded and chopped
1 14½-ounce can no-salt-added stewed tomatoes
1 tablespoon parsley
1 teaspoon cilantro
½ teaspoon ground cumin
½ teaspoon oregano
¼ teaspoon red pepper flakes
1 2½-ounce can sliced black olives, drained and rinsed
2 frozen pie crusts, or homemade pie dough

Per serving:

608 calories
34% of calories from fat
28.9 gm protein
72.8 gm carbohydrates
0 tsp sugar
22.8 gm fat
147.8 mg sodium
40 mg cholesterol

Spray a cookie sheet with baking spray.

In a large nonstick skillet over medium high heat, sauté the turkey, garlic, and onion until the turkey is no longer pink. Drain off any liquid.

Stir in the pepper, tomatoes, parsley, cilantro, cumin, oregano, and red pepper flakes. Cook over medium heat for 15 minutes until most of the liquid is cooked out. Stir in the olives.

Brown 1 pie crust for approximately 5 minutes. Transfer the meat mixture to the shell. Flatten the other pie crust and place it on top. Seal around the edges by pinching with your fingers.

Bake at 400° for 20 to 25 minutes or until golden brown.

Serves 6.

Best bets at the deli

When buying foods at the deli, choose luncheon meats made from turkey or chicken breast meat. Try low-sodium and low-fat cheeses. Pick poultry and meats that have been cooked on a rotisserie, rather than fried chicken, meats served with gravy, or barbecued ribs.

Turkey Topping

½ pound ground raw turkey
12 ounces fresh mushrooms, rinsed clean, halved
4 green onions, white parts thinly sliced
1 13¾-ounce can Pritikin chicken broth
1 cup frozen peas
¼ teaspoon black pepper
2 tablespoons all-purpose flour
½ cup cold water
½ cup red wine
1 teaspoon parsley
2 cups cooked rice (or 4 baked potatoes)
2 tablespoons plain nonfat yogurt

Per serving:

271 calories
7% of calories from fat
23.6 gm protein
32.7 gm carbohydrates
0 tsp sugar
2.4 gm fat
168.9 mg sodium
40.1 mg cholesterol

In a nonstick skillet over medium high heat, brown the turkey for 8 to 10 minutes. Drain.

Add the mushrooms and onions and sauté for 3 to 4 minutes. Add the broth, peas, and pepper, and bring to a boil.

In a container with a cover, combine the flour and water. Shake until blended. Add to the turkey mixture with the wine. Bring to a boil, reduce the heat, and simmer until thickened. Stir frequently.

Stir in the parsley. Serve over rice or potato, and top with a dollop of yogurt. Serves 4.

AaBbCcDdEeFfGgHhIiJjKkLlMmNnOoPpQqRrSsTtUuVvWwXxYyZz

Choose fresh poultry that is skinless. It is always lean.
Compare the labels on ground turkey, as some brands
have almost as much fat as lean ground beef.

Fancy Steamed Salmon

Serve with orzo for a complete meal. This is a fabulous dish that is easy, yet elegant enough for a company meal.

1 tablespoon Promise margarine
½ medium onion, thinly sliced
2 stalks celery, sliced diagonally
2 cups sliced fresh mushrooms
Dash dill weed
½ teaspoon Mrs. Dash
1 pound Alaska salmon fillets
¼ cup white wine
1 6-ounce package frozen snow peas, thawed

Per serving:

145 calories
27% of calories from fat
17.8 gm protein
6.4 gm carbohydrates
0 tsp sugar
4.4 gm fat
118.8 mg sodium
26.0 mg cholesterol

In a nonstick wok or skillet over medium high heat, melt the margarine and sauté the onions, celery, and mushrooms for 4 to 5 minutes, or until the vegetables begin to soften.

Add the dill weed and Mrs. Dash. Continue cooking over low heat for 2 minutes.

Rinse the salmon with cold water and pat dry with a paper towel. Season with Mrs. Dash. Place the salmon over the vegetables and pour the wine over the salmon. Cover and steam for 10 to 15 minutes or until the salmon flakes easily with a fork.

Remove the salmon. Add the snow peas to the vegetable mixture and heat through, about 3 to 4 minutes.

Serves 6.

Gone fishin'

Fish is excellent for low-fat diets. It is usually lower in saturated fat than red meat or poultry and is an excellent source of protein, vitamins, and minerals. Several types of fish are a source of omega-3 fatty acids, which appear to lower blood cholesterol. These fish include tuna, mackerel, salmon, rainbow trout, sardines, and herring. Broil, poach, or bake fish, but do not deep-fry it.

Fish Creole

¼ cup vermouth
1 cup diced onion
1 cup sliced celery with leaves
1 cup diced green pepper
½ cup chopped fresh parsley
2 16-ounce cans no-salt-added whole tomatoes
1 4-ounce can no-salt-added tomato paste
1 teaspoon Mrs. Dash
1 bay leaf
1 teaspoon curry powder
Dash cayenne pepper
¾ pound fresh halibut, cut in 1-inch squares
8 ounces frozen corn
2 cups cooked rice

Per serving:

240 calories
12% of calories from fat
16.9 gm protein
38.9 gm carbohydrates
0 tsp sugar
3.1 gm fat
81.2 mg sodium
30.7 mg cholesterol

In a large, heavy soup pan over medium high, heat bring the vermouth to a boil. Add the onion, celery, and green pepper. Sauté the vegetables for 5 to 6 minutes or until the onions are transparent.

Add the next 7 ingredients to the vegetable mixture. Bring to a gentle boil, then reduce the heat. Cover and simmer for 1 hour to 1 hour and 30 minutes, stirring frequently.

Add the fish and corn and continue to simmer for 15 to 20 minutes. Before serving, remove the bay leaf and stir in the rice.

Serves 6.

More fish facts

Frozen fish is sometimes processed by dipping it into a brine prior to freezing. If you are on a low-sodium diet, always use fresh fish.

Seasonings and flavors for fish include: allspice, basil, bay leaves, caraway seed, cayenne pepper, celery seed, chives, cilantro, curry, dill, garlic, ginger, herbed vinegars, lemon, lime, mace, marjoram, mint, onion, orange, oregano, paprika, parsley, rosemary, saffron, sage, tarragon, and thyme.

Foiled Fish

This is a great dish for a camping trip or a backyard barbecue.

¼ **cup white wine**
1 medium leek, cut into thin 2-inch strips
1 large carrot, cut into thin 2-inch strips
1 tablespoon lemon juice
1 teaspoon tarragon
¾ **pound fish (sole, flounder, or salmon fillets)**
½ **teaspoon Mrs. Dash**
PAM baking spray

Per serving:

217 calories
29% of calories from fat
26.7 gm protein
8.4 gm carbohydrates
0 tsp sugar
7.0 gm fat
218.1 mg sodium
78 mg cholesterol

Preheat the grill.

In a medium nonstick skillet heat the wine over medium heat. Sauté the leek and carrot for 3 minutes. Remove the pan from the heat and add the lemon juice and tarragon. Set aside.

Wash the fish with cold water and pat dry with a paper towel. Spray a large sheet of heavy duty aluminum foil with baking spray. Place the fish on the foil. Sprinkle with Mrs. Dash. Spoon the vegetables on top of the fish. Seal the aluminum foil tightly.

Place the foil on the grill over hot coals. Cook for 7 to 10 minutes, until the fish is done.

Serves 4.

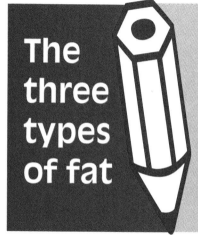

The three types of fat

Saturated fat is found in animal products such as meat, butter, and whole milk, as well as palm and coconut oils. It is directly responsible for raising blood cholesterol levels and should be no more than 10% of a child's daily intake.

The rest of a child's fat intake should come from polyunsaturates such as safflower and corn oils and monounsaturates such as olive and peanut oils. These may have the ability to lower blood cholesterol, but they still have plenty of calories and should each be limited to 10% of a child's calories.

Grilled Halibut

2 tablespoons low-sodium soy sauce
2 tablespoons lemon juice
2 teaspoons brown sugar
1 teaspoon ground ginger
Dash garlic powder
12 ounces halibut

Per serving:

155 calories
26% of calories from fat
24.3 gm fat
2.7 gm carbohydrates
0.6 tsp sugar
4.5 gm fat
335 mg sodium
64 mg cholesterol

In a 2-cup liquid measure combine the first 5 ingredients. Pour into a 1-quart sealable freezer bag. Add the halibut and seal the bag. Refrigerate for 1 hour.

Broil on a barbecue grill or in the oven, turning once, until the fish flakes easily with a fork, approximately 4 minutes on each side.

Serves 4.

Marinated Fish Steaks

This is an easy dish to prepare. We enjoy the fish with sweet potatoes and steamed broccoli. Our family favorite!

1 tablespoon low-sodium soy sauce
1 teaspoon garlic powder (or onion powder)
½ teaspoon Mrs. Dash
Juice of 1 small lemon
1 pound swordfish steak (flounder and halibut work well, too)

Per serving:

144 calories
28% of calories from fat
24.3 gm protein
0 gm carbohydrates
0 tsp sugar
4.5 gm fat
115 mg sodium
69 mg cholesterol

In a small bowl combine the soy sauce, garlic powder, Mrs. Dash, and lemon juice. Rinse the fish in cold water and pat dry with a paper towel. Place the fish in a sealable plastic bag. Pour the marinade over the fish and seal the bag. Refrigerate for 1 hour.

Drain off the marinade. Broil the fish on a barbecue grill or in the oven for about 8 to 10 minutes, or until the fish flakes easily with a fork.

Serves 4.

Beef and Barley

We enjoy this dish served with corn bread and fruit salad.

2 cups water
¾ cup hulled barley
¼ cup chopped green pepper
1 carrot, sliced
1 stalk celery, sliced
½ cup diced onion
½ pound very lean ground beef
½ cup no-salt-added green beans, frozen or canned
1 16-ounce can no-salt-added tomatoes

> **Per serving:**
>
> 152 calories
> 9% of calories from fat
> 8.9 gm protein
> 26.5 gm carbohydrates
> 0 tsp sugar
> 1.5 gm fat
> 32.9 mg sodium
> 12 mg cholesterol

In a large saucepan with a tight-fitting lid, combine the water and barley, and bring to a boil. Cover, reduce the heat, and simmer for 30 minutes.

While cooking the barley, in a large nonstick frying pan combine the green pepper, carrot, celery, onion, and ground beef. Over medium high heat brown the ground beef and vegetables until the meat is no longer pink. Drain.

When the barley is cooked, add the green beans, tomatoes and their juice, and the meat mixture to the barley and bring to a boil. Cover and simmer for 30 minutes, stirring occasionally.

Serves 6.

Fat grams per 5-ounce raw serving of beef and pork:

ground beef, extra lean	24	sirloin, choice	30
ground beef, lean	30	T-bone steak	37
ground beef, regular	38	pork spareribs	34
3 beef hot dogs	41	pork top loin	37

Corny Beef

1 teaspoon olive oil
½ pound sirloin steak, thinly sliced
1 medium onion, chopped
½ teaspoon thyme
½ cup dry red wine
2 14½-ounce cans no-salt-added stewed tomatoes
1 16-ounce can no-salt-added whole kernel sweet corn
   (or 2 cups frozen corn)
2 cups cooked white rice

Per serving:

212 calories
19% of calories from fat
16.1 gm protein
28.4 gm carbohydrates
0 tsp sugar
4.4 gm fat
38.5 mg sodium
34.7 mg cholesterol

In a nonstick skillet heat the oil over medium heat. Sauté the meat, onion, and thyme until the meat is browned. Add the wine and bring to a boil. Reduce the heat and simmer for 7 to 8 minutes.

Add the tomatoes to the meat mixture. Cover, reduce the heat, and simmer for 15 minutes. Add the corn and cook another 5 minutes uncovered, until heated through.

Stir in the rice. Serve hot.

Serves 6.

Be a beef expert

Pay close attention when considering prepackaged ground beef. Government regulations allow up to 30% added fat. Select those that are labeled 80% lean, or shop in places that will grind lean chuck or top sirloin to order for you.

Broil hamburgers rather than fry them. This will allow the internal fat to drip off. Also, try making chickenburgers, turkey burgers, and vealburgers instead of hamburgers. Add herbs, spices, and salt-free seasonings to make them interesting.

Tamale Pie

½ **pound very lean ground beef**
½ **cup chopped onion**
½ **cup chopped green pepper**
Dash garlic powder
1 16-ounce can no-salt-added whole tomatoes, crushed
1 14-ounce can no-salt-added stewed tomatoes
1 16-ounce can Rosarita Vegetarian Refried Beans
1 cup frozen corn
3 green onions, sliced
½ **teaspoon cilantro**
¼ **teaspoon ground cumin**
Corn bread batter (see recipe, p. 59)
1 cup shredded low-fat, low-sodium cheddar cheese

Per serving:
242 calories
13% of calories from fat
12.5 gm protein
42.6 gm carbohydrates
0 tsp sugar
3.6 gm fat
336.7 mg sodium
16 mg cholesterol

In a large nonstick skillet combine the ground beef, onion, green pepper, and garlic powder. Over medium high heat brown the ground beef and vegetables until the meat is no longer pink. Drain. Add the remaining ingredients except the corn bread batter and cheese. Prepare the corn bread batter according to the recipe. Stir in the cheese.

Spoon the meat mixture into a 13 x 9 x 2-inch baking dish. Spread the corn bread mixture over the meat, covering it completely.

Bake at 375° for 30 to 35 minutes. Let the pie stand for 10 minutes.

Refrigerate leftovers. Reheats well in the microwave for individual servings. Serves 10.

AaBbCcDdEeFfGgHhIiJjKkLlMmNnOoPpQqRrSsTtUuVvWwXxYyZz

When your children accompany you to the supermarket, teach them to compare nutritional labels of the various brands. This will certainly provide surprises for them. For instance, some brands of refried beans contain lard. Have your children help in the search for vegetarian-style refried beans.

Polish Kielbasa Casserole

This is not often served because of its high fat and cholesterol content.

4 large red potatoes, peeled and thinly sliced
1 tablespoon Promise margarine
2 tablespoons all-purpose flour
2 cups skim milk
¼ teaspoon black pepper
8 ounces kielbasa, thinly sliced
PAM baking spray
½ white onion, thinly sliced
8 ounces shredded green cabbage

Per serving:

345 calories
58% of calories from fat
14.7 gm protein
21.6 gm carbohydrates
0 tsp sugar
22.3 gm fat
899.6 mg sodium
49.3 mg cholesterol

In a large bowl soak the potatoes in cold water. In a medium saucepan melt the margarine over medium heat. Stir in the flour with a wire whisk. Cook for one minute, then gradually add the milk, ⅛ cup at a time, stirring constantly with the wire whisk. Continue cooking over medium heat, stirring constantly, until the sauce thickens. Add the pepper and set aside.

In a nonstick frying pan cook the kielbasa until lightly browned. Drain and pat the kielbasa dry with paper towel. Set aside.

Spray a 3-quart casserole with baking spray. Drain the potatoes. Place ⅓ of the potato slices on the bottom of the casserole. Top with ½ of the onion slices, ½ of the cabbage, then ½ of the kielbasa. Spread ⅓ of the white sauce over all. Repeat the layers, ending with potato slices, then sauce.

Cover the casserole. Bake at 350° for 1 hour and 30 minutes, or until the potatoes are done. Check the casserole after 1 hour and 15 minutes to be sure it is not drying out.

Serves 6.

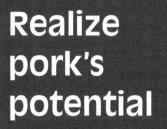

Realize pork's potential

Seasonings and flavors for pork include: apple cider, black beans, brown sugar, caraway seeds, cardamom, cilantro, cloves, dill, garlic, ginger, honey, jalapeño pepper, lemon and orange marmalade, molasses, onion, red wine vinegar, rosemary, saffron, sage, tarragon, and thyme.

Pork Chops

These taste great over rice or orzo.

PAM baking spray
4 pork chop tenderloins (about 1½ pounds)
1 cup chopped tomatoes
½ cup diced onion
Mrs. Dash

Per serving:

271 calories
46% of calories from fat
31.7 gm protein
3.2 gm carbohydrates
0 tsp sugar
13.8 gm fat
72.8 mg sodium
100 mg cholesterol

Spray a 2-quart casserole with baking spray. In a nonstick skillet brown the pork chops. Place a layer of tomatoes and onions in the bottom of the casserole. Add the pork chops, lightly season with Mrs. Dash, then top with the remaining tomatoes and onions. Cover with foil. Bake at 325° for 35 to 40 minutes, or until the chops are tender and cooked inside, but not dry.
Serves 4.

Look at your LDL's & HDL's

Cholesterol is a type of fatty substance that the body needs to manufacture cell membranes and hormones. Two main kinds of cholesterol circulate in the bloodstream: low-density lipoproteins (LDLs) that are considered bad because they carry cholesterol to the body cells; and high-density lipoproteins (HDLs) that are considered good because they carry cholesterol away from body cells and may help prevent the buildup of fatty deposits on artery walls.

Serum cholesterol is the level of cholesterol found in the blood. This is the number referred to in cholesterol tests. Dietary cholesterol is obtained from food, particularly animal products such as meat, dairy, and eggs. Plants do not contain cholesterol.

Too much dietary cholesterol can raise serum cholesterol.

Rice and Broccoli Bake

Serve with orange slices and banana bread for a great meal.

2¼ cups cold water
1 cup brown rice
¼ cup cooking sherry (or Madeira for a different flavor)
½ large white onion, chopped
1 clove garlic, minced
½ pound sliced fresh mushrooms
1½ pounds broccoli, bottom stalks removed, thinly
   sliced
1 stalk celery, chopped
¼ teaspoon dill weed
½ teaspoon Italian seasoning
½ cup chopped fresh parsley (or 2 tablespoons dried)
¼ cup unsalted cashews
PAM baking spray
3 ounces low-fat, low-sodium mild cheddar cheese, grated
¼ cup Parmesan cheese
2 cups plain nonfat yogurt, halved

Per serving:

138 calories
24% of calories from fat
8.9 gm protein
17.5 gm carbohydrates
0 tsp sugar
3.8 gm fat
135 mg sodium
3.1 mg cholesterol

In a large saucepan with a tight-fitting lid, combine the water and rice and bring to a boil. Cover, reduce the heat, and simmer for 45 minutes, or until the water is absorbed. Set aside.

In a nonstick skillet heat the sherry and sauté the onions and garlic for 7 to 10 minutes. Add the mushrooms, broccoli, and celery. Stir frequently until the broccoli starts to change color, about 4 to 5 minutes. Remove from the heat and add the dill weed, Italian seasoning, parsley, cashews, and 1 cup of yogurt.

Coat a 2-quart baking dish with baking spray. Place the rice on the bottom, pour the vegetable mixture over the rice, sprinkle the cheeses over the vegetables, and top evenly with dollops of the remaining yogurt.

Bake at 350° for 20 to 30 minutes.

Serves 10.

The Bullfighter's Rice

Adults may top this with salsa for added flavor.

2¼ cups cold water
1 cup brown rice
¼ cup skim milk
2 cups low-fat, low-sodium cottage cheese
¼ cup diced white onion
1 15-ounce can no-salt-added kidney beans, rinsed and drained
6 black olives, sliced
1 cup grated low-fat, low-sodium Monterey Jack cheese

Per serving:

247 calories
25% of calories from fat
21.4 gm protein
25 gm carbohydrates
0 tsp sugar
6.9 mg fat
544 mg sodium
23.5 mg cholesterol

In a saucepan with a tight lid combine the water and rice. Bring the water to a boil. Cover, reduce the heat, and simmer for 45 minutes. Let the rice sit for an additional 10 minutes.

Spray a 2-quart baking dish lightly with baking spray. In a small bowl mix the milk with the cottage cheese. In a separate bowl combine the rice, onion, beans, and olives. With ⅓ of the rice mixture, cover the bottom of the baking dish. Layer with 2 ounces of cheese and ⅓ of the cottage cheese mixture. Repeat the layers, ending with rice. Bake at 350° for 30 minutes.

Sprinkle a little cheese on top during the last 5 minutes of baking.

Serves 6.

AaBbCcDdEeFfGgHhIiJjKkLlMmNnOoPpQqRrSsTtUuVvWwXxYyZz

Salt is an acquired taste. Hopefully, kids who do not learn to salt everything as children will grow into adults who are not in the habit of eating a lot of salt. Ideally, a child should not have more than 2,000 milligrams of sodium daily. Read labels carefully—if a serving of soup contains 1,000 milligrams, that's half of a day's allotment.

Easy Bean Burritos

6 6-inch corn tortillas
1 12-ounce can no-salt-added kidney beans,
  rinsed and drained
1 cup grated low-fat low-sodium mild cheddar cheese
1 cup salsa
1 cup plain nonfat yogurt

Steam the tortillas until pliable. On each tortilla spoon 1½ ounces of beans, ½ ounce of cheese, 1 tablespoon of the salsa, and 1 tablespoon of yogurt. Roll up the tortillas and place seamside down in a baking pan. Pour the remaining salsa over the burritos. Bake at 425° for 4 to 6 minutes, until thoroughly heated.
    Serves 6.

Per serving:

179 calories
32% of calories from fat
10.9 gm protein
21.5 gm carbohydrates
0 tsp sugar
6.5 gm fat
198.9 mg sodium
22 mg cholesterol

Tortilla and Black Bean Casserole

We enjoy this meal with pink grapefruit.

¼ **cup white wine**
1 **medium onion, chopped**
1 **clove garlic, minced (or ¼ teaspoon garlic powder)**
½ **green bell pepper, seeded and chopped**
½ **red bell pepper, seeded and chopped**
¾ **cup salsa (see recipe, p. 64)**
½ **teaspoon ground cumin**
1 **15-ounce can no-salt-added black beans, drained**
1 **14½-ounce can no-salt-added stewed tomatoes**
PAM baking spray
8 **6-inch corn tortillas**
1½ **cups shredded low-fat, low-sodium Monterey Jack cheese**
4 **tablespoons plain nonfat yogurt**

Per serving:
275 calories
27% of calories from fat
16.4 gm protein
35.6 gm carbohydrates
0 tsp sugar
8.4 gm fat
201 mg sodium
15.0 mg cholesterol

In a large nonstick skillet bring the wine to a boil over medium high heat. Add the onion and garlic and sauté for 5 minutes. Add the peppers and sauté for an additional 3 minutes. Add a little wine if necessary so the vegetables do not stick to the pan. Add the salsa, cumin, beans, and tomatoes. Cook for 5 minutes over medium heat. Remove from the heat and set aside.

Spray a 13 x 9 x 2-inch baking dish with baking spray. Spoon 1 cup of the bean mixture in the bottom of the prepared dish and distribute evenly. Arrange 4 tortillas in a single layer over the beans. Top with ¾ cup of cheese. Spoon ½ cup of bean mixture over each tortilla and spread with a spatula to distribute evenly. Arrange the remaining 4 tortillas over the bean mixture. Top with the remaining bean mixture. Reserve the remaining cheese.

Cover the pan with foil. Bake at 350° for 30 minutes. Remove the foil. Sprinkle the remaining cheese over the top. Return to the oven uncovered and bake for an additional 5 minutes, or until the cheese is melted. Remove from the oven and let the casserole stand for 5 minutes before serving. Top with a dollop of plain nonfat yogurt.

Serves 8.

Tofu Burgers

My children love these burgers. They do fall apart easily, so I do not recommend cooking them on the grill or using with buns.

15 ounces tofu, drained, mashed, and dried
½ cup chopped onion
½ cup chopped red bell pepper
2 egg whites
¼ cup oat bran
2 tablespoons Parmesan cheese
1 teaspoon parsley
½ teaspoon Mrs. Dash
¼ teaspoon celery seed
Dash pepper
Dash garlic powder
3 tablespoons all-purpose flour
1 tablespoon olive oil

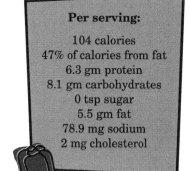

Per serving:

104 calories
47% of calories from fat
6.3 gm protein
8.1 gm carbohydrates
0 tsp sugar
5.5 gm fat
78.9 mg sodium
2 mg cholesterol

In a large bowl combine all of the ingredients except the flour and olive oil. Shape into 4 patties. Refrigerate the patties on a plate for 30 minutes.

Dust a sheet of waxed paper or pastry cloth with the flour. Place the patties on the flour and turn to coat. In a large nonstick skillet heat the oil over medium heat. Cook the patties for 7 minutes on each side. (They can also be broiled.)

Serves 4.

AaBbCcDdEeFfGgHhIiJjKkLlMmNnOoPpQqRrSsTtUuVvWwXxYyZz

Tofu has 6 grams of fat per 5-ounce raw serving. Tofu can be used as a meat substitute in most ground beef recipes and a cheese replacement in dishes using cottage, cream, or ricotta cheese. Try tofu hot dogs on the grill. Tofu can be cubed to add to chef's salads, too.

Guacamole Topping for Veggie Burritos

2 ripe avocados, peeled and pitted
¼ cup plain nonfat yogurt
½ teaspoon chili powder
1 tablespoon lemon juice
½ tomato, chopped

In a medium bowl mash the avocado. Stir in the yogurt, chili powder, lemon juice, and tomato. Cover and refrigerate until ready to use.

Per serving:

87 calories
80% of calories from fat
1.5 gm protein
4.6 gm carbohydrates
0 tsp sugar
7.7 gm fat
10.3 mg sodium
0.2 mg cholesterol

Q

True or false: To control cholesterol, you should only eat products labeled "cholesterol-free"?

False. The total amount of fat in a product, particularly saturated fat, will affect blood cholesterol. A product that claims to have no cholesterol may still have fat, as well as sugar and sodium.

Veggie Burrito

This recipe is one of our all-time favorites. It's a meal in itself.

¼ cup white wine
1 clove garlic, minced
¼ cup diced red onion
¼ cup diced white onion
6 black olives, thinly sliced
1 large tomato, peeled, seeded, and chopped
1 carrot, shredded
1 medium zucchini, cut in ½-inch slices
¾ pound mushrooms, rinsed and sliced
½ green pepper, diced
½ teaspoon chili powder
½ teaspoon oregano
¼ teaspoon ground cumin
8 whole-wheat tortillas
1 16-ounce can Rosarita Vegetarian Refried Beans
Guacamole Topping (see recipe, p. 116)
¾ cup grated low-fat, low-sodium Monterey Jack cheese
Grated Monterey Jack cheese for garnish
1½ cups shredded lettuce

Per serving:

141 calories
23% of calories from fat
8.8 gm protein
20.9 gm carbohydrates
0 tsp sugar
3.6 gm fat
358.4 mg sodium
7.5 mg cholesterol

In a large nonstick saucepan heat the wine over medium high heat and sauté the garlic and onions until soft, approximately 5 minutes. Add the olives, tomato, carrot, zucchini, mushrooms, pepper, chili powder, oregano, and cumin. Bring to a boil. Reduce the heat and simmer for 10 minutes. Drain.

Wrap the tortillas in foil and warm in a 350° oven for 10 minutes. This softens them and makes them pliable.

In a small saucepan warm the refried beans over low heat. Stir in the cheese, then add the bean mixture to the vegetable mixture. Spread about ¼ cup of vegetable mixture on each tortilla. Top with about ¼ cup of guacamole. Place the burritos seam-side down on serving plates. Top with cheese and shredded lettuce. The guacamole topping is high in fat, and you may prefer to use plain nonfat yogurt.

Serves 8.

Vegetarian Stir-Fry

2 teaspoons sesame seeds
⅔ cup Pritikin chicken broth
2 tablespoons low-sodium soy sauce
2 teaspoons cornstarch
2 tablespoons water
2 teaspoons sesame oil
½ teaspoon ground ginger
¼ pound fresh mushrooms, rinsed and sliced
2 cups small broccoli flowerettes
1 carrot, sliced
3 green onions, white parts sliced diagonally
1 small zucchini, sliced
1 15-ounce can baby corn, drained and rinsed
2½ cups cooked white rice
½ cup raw unsalted cashews

Per serving:

151 calories
15% of calories from fat
6.9 gm protein
27.6 gm carbohydrates
0 tsp sugar
2.5 gm fat
83.2 mg sodium
0 mg cholesterol

In a small nonstick frying pan toast sesame seeds over medium heat for 5 minutes, until lightly browned, stirring frequently.

In a 2-cup measure, combine the sesame seeds, chicken broth, and soy sauce. Set the sauce aside. In a small bowl combine the cornstarch and the water, mixing until smooth. Set aside.

Heat a wok over high heat. Add the oil, coating all sides. Add the ginger and stir. Add the mushrooms, broccoli, carrot, green onions, and zucchini. Stir-fry for 1 minute. Add the sauce, cooking for 2 minutes. Add the baby corn, cover, and cook for 2 more minutes. Add the cornstarch mixture and cook, stirring, until the sauce boils. Serve the vegetables over the cooked rice. Top with cashews.

Serves 6.

Smart substitution

If you do not have low-sodium soy sauce on hand, you can dilute regular soy sauce by mixing 1 part water to 1 part soy sauce..

Vegetables

Steamed Asparagus

This is great with grilled fish and potatoes.

½ to ¾ pound asparagus (or Brussels sprouts)

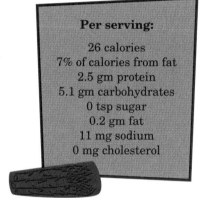

Rinse the asparagus and break off the tough ends. In the bottom of a steamer bring a small amount of water to a boil. Place the asparagus in the top of the steamer. Cover and steam for 8 to 10 minutes, or until slightly softened in the center.
    Serves 4.

Per serving:

26 calories
7% of calories from fat
2.5 gm protein
5.1 gm carbohydrates
0 tsp sugar
0.2 gm fat
11 mg sodium
0 mg cholesterol

Italian Beans

½ cup Pritikin chicken broth
2 cups frozen no-salt-added beans
½ cup chopped canned no-salt-added tomatoes
2 teaspoons Parmesan cheese

In a medium saucepan bring the chicken broth to a boil. Add the frozen beans and cook according to the package directions.
    When the beans are done, add the tomatoes and Parmesan cheese. Heat over low heat for 30 seconds.
    Serves 4.

Per serving:

129 calories
11% of calories from fat
10.7 gm protein
21.5 gm carbohydrates
0 tsp sugar
1.6 gm fat
105.2 mg sodium
9.4 mg cholesterol

Broccoli and Tofu

My young son thinks tofu is chicken, and that's fine with me. He loves it.

1 teaspoon sesame oil
¼ cup diced onion (or 3 green onions, sliced diagonally)
8 ounces firm tofu, drained and cut into ½-inch cubes
2 tablespoons low-sodium soy sauce
1 tablespoon rice vinegar
½ teaspoon ginger
2 cups broccoli flowerettes
1 medium red bell pepper, diced
1½ cups mushrooms
1 cup sliced zucchini

Per serving:

93 calories
32% of calories from fat
8.1 gm protein
10.9 gm carbohydrates
0 tsp sugar
3.4 gm fat
279.7 mg sodium
0 mg cholesterol

In a nonstick wok or large skillet, heat the oil over medium high heat. Add the onions and stir-fry until soft. Add the tofu and stir-fry until lightly browned.

In a cup mix together the soy sauce, vinegar, and ginger. Add the remaining vegetables and the sauce to the wok. Stir until the vegetables are coated with sauce. Cover and simmer over medium heat 5 to 7 minutes.

Serves 4.

Broccoli can't be beat

Broccoli has almost 3 times as much vitamin C as an orange and almost as much calcium as milk. It is also a good source of vitamins A, E, and K.

Some seasonings and flavors that complement broccoli are: basil, black pepper, caraway seed, low-fat cheddar cheese, curry, dill, garlic, lemon, marjoram, mustard, oregano, Parmesan cheese, tarragon, and thyme.

Green Flowers

The little ones love to sprinkle on the Parmesan cheese and eat the broccoli with their fingers.

½ pound broccoli
1½ tablespoons Parmesan cheese

Wash the broccoli and cut off the tough stems. Cut the broccoli into small flowerets. In the bottom of a steamer bring a small amount of water to a boil. Place the broccoli in the top of the steamer. Cover and steam for 8 to 10 minutes, until the broccoli changes color.
   Top with Parmesan cheese.
   Serves 4.

Per serving:

33 calories
22% of calories from fat
3.6 gm protein
4.4 gm carbohydrates
0 tsp sugar
0.8 gm fat
45.9 mg sodium
1.5 mg cholesterol

Ants on a Log

One of our favorites.

¼ cup creamy peanut butter
4 celery sticks, cleaned, ends cut off, and halved
16 raisins

Spread the peanut butter on the celery sticks. Place 4 to 5 raisins in a row on top of the peanut butter.
   Serves 4.

Per serving:

106 calories
62% of calories from fat
4.7 gm protein
7.3 gm carbohydrates
0 tsp sugar
7.4 gm fat
141.4 mg sodium
0 mg cholesterol

Orange Orange Carrots

½ pound carrots, peeled and sliced ¼-inch thick
½ cup freshly squeezed orange juice
1 tablespoon Promise margarine
1 tablespoon lemon juice
½ teaspoon brown sugar
Dash black pepper

Fill a medium saucepan with water. Bring the water to a rolling boil. Drop the carrots in and continue to boil for 4 to 5 minutes. Drain the carrots. Stir in the remaining ingredients and cook over medium heat until the liquid evaporates. Serve immediately.
   Serves 4.

Per serving:

69 calories
39% of calories from fat
1.0 gm protein
10.4 gm carbohydrates
0.1 tsp sugar
3 gm fat
71.3 mg sodium
0 mg cholesterol

Sweet Carrots

4 medium carrots, thinly sliced
1 cup seedless red grapes, halved
3 tablespoons brown sugar
1 tablespoon cornstarch
¼ cup water
3 tablespoons dry white wine

Per serving:

75 calories
2% of calories from fat
0.8 gm protein
18.0 gm carbohydrates
1.7 tsp sugar
0.2 gm fat
27.8 mg sodium
0 mg cholesterol

In a medium saucepan cover the carrots with water. Bring the water to a boil. Cover, reduce the heat, and simmer for 7 to 8 minutes. Drain. Place the carrots in a serving bowl and add the grapes.
   In a small saucepan combine the brown sugar and cornstarch, mixing well. Stir in the water and wine with a wire whisk. Stir constantly over medium heat until it just begins to thicken. Pour the sauce over the carrot mixture and toss gently. Serve immediately.
   Serves 6.

Mashed Potatoes

An old-time favorite that is very healthy without butter.

4 to 5 medium new red potatoes
½ cup skim milk

Per serving:

92 calories
2% of calories from fat
3.5 gm protein
19.5 gm carbohydrates
0 tsp sugar
0.2 gm fat
17.8 mg sodium
0.5 mg cholesterol

Peel the potatoes and place them in a bowl of cold water. This keeps them from turning brown.

Fill a large pot with water. Bring the water to a boil. Add the potatoes and boil for 45 minutes, or until soft inside when poked with a fork. Transfer the potatoes to a medium bowl. Mash with a potato masher or fork. Add the milk and beat with an electric mixer until smooth. Add a little more milk if necessary.

Keep the potatoes warm until needed by covering the bowl and placing it in a pan of hot water.

Serves 4.

Mushroom Potato Pie

4 large red potatoes
¼ cup skim milk
¼ cup white wine
2 cups sliced fresh mushrooms
½ cup diced onion
1 teaspoon lemon juice
⅛ teaspoon pepper
PAM baking spray
¾ cup plain nonfat yogurt

Per serving:

85 calories
3% of calories from fat
3.8 gm protein
16.5 gm carbohydrates
0 tsp sugar
0.3 gm fat
27.8 mg sodium
0.7 mg cholesterol

In a large saucepan cover the potatoes with water. Bring the water to a boil. Cook the potatoes until soft. Peel. In a medium bowl mash the potatoes and add ¼ cup of milk. Beat for 1 to 2 minutes with an electric mixer.

In a nonstick skillet heat the wine and sauté the mushrooms and onions until soft. Add the lemon juice and pepper.

Spray a 2-quart casserole with baking spray. Spread half of the potatoes in the bottom of the prepared casserole. Spread the mushroom mixture over the potatoes and spread the yogurt over all. Top with the remaining potatoes. Bake at 350° for 35 to 40 minutes.

Serves 6.

Parslied Boiled and Baked Potatoes

Great as leftovers. Sprinkle with ¼ cup of low-fat grated cheddar cheese, cover with waxed paper, and microwave on high for 2 minutes.

6 small to medium red potatoes (1 pound)
PAM baking spray
1 teaspoon dried parsley flakes
1 teaspoon Mrs. Dash
2 teaspoons Promise margarine
1 teaspoon lemon juice

Per serving:
78 calories
22% of calories from fat
1.8 gm protein
13.6 gm carbohydrates
0 tsp sugar
1.9 gm fat
23.7 mg sodium
0 mg cholesterol

Peel the potatoes and place them in a bowl of cold water. Fill a saucepan with water. Bring the water to a boil. Add the potatoes and boil for 45 minutes, or until soft inside when poked with a fork.

Spray a 2-quart casserole lightly with baking spray. Place the potatoes in the prepared casserole. Sprinkle with parsley and Mrs. Dash. Dot with margarine and sprinkle with lemon juice. Cover with foil. Bake at 300° for 15 minutes.

Serves 4.

Plain Potatoes

Serve with margarine and a little pepper, or try a dollop of plain nonfat yogurt instead. A sure-fire favorite.

4 medium potatoes (red, white, Idaho, or sweet)

Rinse the potatoes under water and scrub gently with a vegetable brush. Poke 2 or 3 times with a fork.

   Place the potatoes on a paper towel in the microwave. Microwave on high for 10 to 12 minutes, until the potatoes begin to soften. Remove from the microwave and wrap in aluminum foil. Let the potatoes rest for 10 minutes.

   Serves 4.

Per serving:

81 calories
1% of calories from fat
2.4 gm protein
18 gm carbohydrates
0 tsp sugar
0.1 gm fat
2 mg sodium
0 mg cholesterol

Steer clear of fats

Serve vegetables without heavy sauces, gravies, and dressings. They add lots of fat and calories and interfere with the flavor of the vegetable rather than enhance it. For example, a large serving of steamed broccoli has about 50 calories, but with 2 tablespoons of Hollandaise sauce it jumps to 350 calories.

   A few heaping tablespoons of sour cream on a baked potato have more saturated fat than a small filet mignon.

Potatoes and Cabbage

1 tablespoon margarine
1 8-ounce potato, sliced
½ cup chopped yellow bell pepper
½ cup chopped red bell pepper
½ cup chopped onion
2 tablespoons white wine
½ head cabbage, rinsed in cold water and shredded
2 tablespoons water
½ teaspoon Mrs. Dash

Per serving:

72 calories
25% of calories from fat
2 gm protein
12.5 gm carbohydrates
0 tsp sugar
2.0 gm fat
34.8 mg sodium
0 mg cholesterol

In a large nonstick skillet melt the margarine over medium heat. Sauté the potato slices in the margarine for 3 to 4 minutes. Add the peppers and onion. Stir-fry for an additional 3 to 4 minutes. Add the white wine as needed to keep the vegetables from burning. Add the cabbage and water and season with Mrs. Dash. Cover and steam for 20 minutes, stirring occasionally, until the potatoes are soft.

Serves 6.

Don't despair!

If your child does not eat green vegetables, try carrots, squash, corn, beets, or sweet potatoes. These are less bitter tasting.

If your child does not eat any vegetables, try bananas, apples, or pears. They offer many of the same nutrients as vegetables. Also, apricots, mangoes, peaches, and nectarines are excellent sources of vitamin A. Guava, grapefruit, oranges, strawberries, and tangerines are excellent sources of vitamin C.

Baked Tomatoes

3 medium tomatoes, sliced in ⅓-inch slices
⅛ teaspoon garlic powder
¼ cup shredded Parmesan cheese
1 tablespoon fresh parsley
1 tablespoon minced ripe olives
⅛ teaspoon black pepper

Place the tomato slices on a cookie sheet. Sprinkle with garlic powder. Broil 7 inches from the heat for 2 to 3 minutes. Top with the remaining ingredients and broil for about 1 minute more, until the cheese melts.
    Serves 4.

Per serving:

38 calories
30% of calories from fat
2.6 gm protein
4.5 gm carbohydrates
0 tsp sugar
1.3 gm fat
74.6 mg sodium
3 mg cholesterol

Vegetable Put-Together

A good dish with baked chicken and potatoes.

PAM baking spray
1 yellow squash, sliced in ½-inch slices
1 zucchini squash, sliced in 2 x ½-inch strips
1 yellow pepper, sliced in ¼-inch rings
1 red pepper, sliced in ¼-inch rings
½ pound fresh mushrooms, sliced
¼ red onion, diced
2 teaspoons olive oil
¼ teaspoon thyme
¼ teaspoon basil
Dash black pepper

Per serving:

41 calories
37% of calories from fat
1.7 gm protein
5.9 gm carbohydrates
0 tsp sugar
1.7 gm fat
10.5 mg sodium
0 mg cholesterol

Spray a nonstick roasting pan with baking spray. In the prepared pan combine all of the ingredients, stirring well to coat the vegetables with oil and seasonings. Bake at 375° for 15 to 20 minutes, stirring frequently.
    Serves 6.

Tomato Rice

This is a great side dish and a good accompaniment to burritos or trout.

1 teaspoon olive oil (or 1 tablespoon chicken broth)
¼ cup diced onion
2 cups Pritikin chicken broth
¼ cup water
1 cup long-grain white rice
2 tomatoes, peeled, seeded, and chopped (or
   1 16-ounce can)
8 black olives, sliced
1 teaspoon basil
Dash pepper
Dash garlic powder (optional)

Per serving:

92 calories
20% of calories from fat
2.4 gm protein
16.8 gm carbohydrates
0 tsp sugar
2.0 gm fat
87.4 mg sodium
0 mg cholesterol

In a nonstick skillet heat the oil over medium high heat and sauté the onion for 5 to 7 minutes or until transparent.

In a large saucepan with a tight-fitting lid, combine the chicken broth, ¼ cup water, the rice, and onions. Bring the mixture to a boil. Cover, reduce the heat, and simmer for 15 minutes.

Meanwhile, fill a separate saucepan with water. Bring the water to a boil. Add the tomatoes and boil for 1 minute. Remove the tomatoes from the pan with a long-handled fork. Peel, remove the seeds, and chop.

When the rice is done, stir in the black olives, basil, pepper, garlic powder if desired, and the tomatoes. Cover and set aside for 5 minutes before serving.

Serves 6.

Some vegetable facts:

• Cabbage, cauliflower, and broccoli are thought to contain chemicals that protect against cancer.

• Dried beans have protein without much fat and contain soluble fiber that helps lower cholesterol.

• Broccoli has almost 3 times as much vitamin C as an orange.

Wild Rice

This dish goes well with chicken or fish.

3 cups water
½ cup wild rice, rinsed in a strainer under cool water
½ cup brown rice
¼ cup white wine
½ medium onion, chopped
4 ounces fresh mushrooms, rinsed and sliced
PAM baking spray
½ cup low-fat, low-sodium cheddar cheese
1 2½-ounce can sliced black olives, drained
1 14½-ounce can no-salt-added stewed tomatoes

Per serving:
165 calories
20% of calories from fat
6.1 gm protein
27.8 gm carbohydrates
0 tsp sugar
3.8 gm fat
483 mg sodium
6.7 mg cholesterol

Bring the water to a boil. Add the wild rice and brown rice. Cover and cook for 45 to 50 minutes. Drain off any excess water.

In a nonstick skillet bring the wine to a boil over medium high heat. Sauté the onions and mushrooms for 5 minutes.

Spray a 2-quart casserole with baking spray. Add the rice, onion mixture, and remaining ingredients, mixing well. Cover with foil. Bake at 350° for 1 hour.

Serves 6.

Wild world of rice

Wild rice is not a true rice but is used like rice. It has a strong flavor and a chewy texture compared to white rice. It should be rinsed thoroughly before cooking and requires longer cooking time than white rice.

Vegetable Rice

1 cup brown rice
½ pound Chinese cabbage (bok choy)
1 tablespoon olive oil
1 13¾-ounce can Pritikin chicken broth
Dash low-sodium soy sauce
PAM baking spray

Trim the cabbage at the root. Wash thoroughly. Cut the stalks in ½-inch pieces.

Spray a medium saucepan with baking spray. Add the oil and heat over medium high heat. Add the cabbage and sauté, stirring constantly for 1 minute. Add the rice, chicken broth, and soy sauce, and bring to a boil. Reduce the heat to medium low, cover, and cook for 35 to 40 minutes.

Serves 4.

Per serving:

135 calories
24% of calories from fat
3.1 gm protein
23.1 gm carbohydrates
0 tsp sugar
3.6 gm fat
77 mg sodium
0 mg cholesterol

The scoop on rice

White rice has been milled to remove the outer bran. Most white rice has been enriched to replace the lost nutrients. Brown rice has had only the outer hull removed, leaving the bran layer. Rice should be stored at room temperature in a cool, dry place. Once the package has been opened, store the rice in an airtight container. White rice will keep indefinitely, but brown rice should be refrigerated if it is to be kept for more than 6 months.

Yellow Rice

Great with pork chops.

1 teaspoon olive oil
1 cup uncooked long-grain white rice
½ clove garlic, minced (or a dash of garlic powder)
⅛ teaspoon saffron threads
1 13¾-ounce can Pritikin chicken broth
¼ teaspoon Mrs. Dash

Per serving:

71 calories
10% of calories from fat
1.8 protein
14.1 gm carbohydrates
0 tsp sugar
0.8 gm fat
46.7 mg sodium
0 mg cholesterol

In a medium saucepan heat the oil over medium heat. Add the rice, garlic, and saffron. Sauté for 2 minutes. Stir in the chicken broth and bring to a boil. Cover, reduce the heat, and simmer 15 to 17 minutes.
Serves 6.

Seasoning suggestions

Some seasonings and flavors that complement rice are: basil, black pepper, cheese, chives, cinnamon, currants, dill, garlic, lemon, mint, nuts, olives, onion, orange, parsley, raisins, saffron, tarragon, thyme, and tomato (see the recipe on page 129).

Saffron, the most expensive spice in the world, is made from the hand-picked dried yellow stigmas of crocus. Purchase saffron threads, rather than powder. The powder loses its pungency quickly, and is often diluted with less expensive seasonings.

Desserts and Treats

Apple Crisp or Pie Filling

3 large Red Delicious apples, peeled and sliced
1 6-ounce can frozen unsweetened apple juice
  concentrate
1½ tablespoons cornstarch
⅛ cup water
1 teaspoon cinnamon or nutmeg
4 teaspoons margarine (for pie filling)
PAM baking spray

Per serving of filling:

109 calories
23% of calories from fat
0.1 gm protein
21.9 gm carbohydrates
0 tsp sugar
2.8 gm fat
31.2 mg sodium
0 mg cholesterol

In a large saucepan combine the apples and apple juice. Bring the juice to a boil. Reduce the heat, cover, and simmer for 5 minutes.

In a cup dissolve the cornstarch in the water. Stir the cornstarch mixture into the apple mixture and return to a boil. Reduce the heat, cover, and simmer for 15 minutes. Stir in the cinnamon or nutmeg.

For Apple Pie, prepare the pie crust according to the Whole-Wheat Pie Crust recipe (see recipe, p. 135). Fill the crust with the apple mixture. Dot the filling with margarine. Bake according to the pie crust recipe directions.

For Apple Crisp, prepare the topping according to the Crisp Topping recipe (see recipe, p. 135). Spray a 9-inch square glass baking dish with baking spray. Turn the filling into the prepared dish. Sprinkle with topping mixture. Bake according to the topping recipe directions.

Makes enough filling for 6 servings.

Crisp Topping

Serve the crisp warm with a dollop of vanilla nonfat yogurt.

½ cup Quaker Old-Fashioned Oats
3 tablespoons all-purpose flour
3 tablespoons brown sugar
2 tablespoons Promise margarine, softened

In a medium bowl combine the oats, flour, and brown sugar. With a fork or pastry blender cut the margarine into the dry ingredients. Sprinkle the mixture over the apples. Bake at 375° for 20 minutes. Let the crisp cool for 5 minutes before serving.

Makes topping for an 8-serving crisp.

Per serving of topping:

85 calories
1.1 gm protein
12.1 carbohydrates
1.7 tsp sugar
3.8 gm fat
2.2. mg sodium
0 mg cholesterol

Whole-Wheat Pie Crust

1¼ cups all-purpose flour
¾ cup whole-wheat flour
5 teaspoons wheat germ
Pinch salt
⅓ cup corn oil
⅓ cup boiling water

Combine dry ingredients. Stir in the oil and water, and mix until moistened. Gather the pastry into a ball. Divide into ¾ and ¼ portions. Roll out the pastry between 2 sheets of waxed paper to about ⅛-inch thickness. Place the large portion in a pie shell. Cut 1-inch strips from the remaining pastry. Fill the crust with Apple Pie Filling and top with the strips of pastry, making a lattice. Bake at 350° for 35 to 40 minutes.

Makes crust for an 8-serving pie.

Per serving of crust:

221 calories
4.8 gm protein
29.4 gm carbohydrates
0 tsp sugar
9.7 gm fat
0.9 mg sodium
0 mg cholesterol

Brown Rice Pudding

½ cup brown rice
1¼ cups water
½ cup raisins
1 teaspoon cinnamon
1 3½-ounce package vanilla instant pudding
2 cups skim milk
½ cup Dream Whip Lite
1 cup fruit cocktail

Per serving:

208 calories
6% of calories from fat
4.2 gm protein
46.6 gm carbohydrates
3.8 tsp sugar
1.5 gm fat
157.3 mg sodium
3.3 mg cholesterol

In a medium saucepan with a tight-fitting lid, combine the rice and water. Bring the water to a boil over high heat. Cover and reduce the heat to medium low. Cook for 40 minutes, or until the water is absorbed. Remove from the heat and let the rice stand for 15 minutes.

Stir the raisins and cinnamon into the rice mixture.

In a medium bowl combine the pudding mix and milk, stirring until well combined. In a microwave-safe dish combine the pudding mixture and the rice mixture. Microwave on high for 8 to 10 minutes, or until the mixture comes to a boil. (You may also do this on your stove over medium heat, stirring frequently, until the mixture comes to a boil.) Cover and refrigerate until chilled all the way through.

Add the Dream Whip and fruit cocktail, and serve.

Serves 6.

Some nutritional alternatives when your child doesn't like milk or dairy products:

- *For calcium: yogurt, cheese, eggs, broccoli, beans*

- *For vitamin A: carrots, squash, peaches, watermelon, cheese*

- *For vitamin D: egg yolks, tuna, liver, salmon*

- *For protein: eggs, chicken, beef, lentils*

- *For riboflavin: meat, dark green vegetables, eggs, whole-grain cereal*

- *Some dishes to consider: healthy varieties of pizza, pudding, creamy soups, pancakes*

Happy Hearts

Great for Valentine's Day dessert.

⅓ **cup Promise margarine, softened**
¼ **cup honey**
⅔ **cups Quaker Old-Fashioned Oats**
⅓ **cup nonfat powdered milk**
4 teaspoons water
¾ **cup all-purpose flour**
1½ **teaspoons low-sodium baking powder**

> **Per cookie:**
>
> 119 calories
> 48% of calories from fat
> 2.1 gm protein
> 13.8 gm carbohydrates
> 0 tsp sugar
> 6.4 gm fat
> 10.5 mg sodium
> 0.3 mg cholesterol

In a large bowl cream together the margarine and honey with an electric mixer. Add the oats, milk, and water, mixing well.

In a small bowl combine the flour and baking powder. Slowly beat the dry ingredients into the honey mixture. Cover the bowl with a plate or plastic wrap. Chill in the refrigerator for 1 hour.

On a lightly floured or sugared surface, roll out the dough to ¼-inch thickness. Let the children cut out their own hearts with 2-inch heart-shaped cookie cutters and place them on the baking sheet 1 inch apart. Bake at 325° for 10 to 12 minutes, or until lightly browned.

Makes 1 dozen cookies.

A close look at sugar

The average American consumes 129 pounds of sugar each year. In principle, sugar is not harmful. In practice, it has no nutritional value other than calories, and it keeps us away from more nutritional foods. It is also the leading cause of tooth decay.

There are 40 calories in a tablespoon of sugar. You may reduce the amount of sugar in your favorite recipes by ¼ to ½, and replace it with ½ as much nonfat powdered milk as omitted sugar.

Try to limit beverages that contain sugar to mealtimes. Between meals drink water.

Oatmeal Cookies

2 egg whites
1 teaspoon vanilla extract
1 cup raisins
¾ cup Promise margarine
¾ cup packed brown sugar
¼ cup sugar
1 cup unbleached all-purpose flour
½ cup whole-wheat flour
2 cups Quaker Old-Fashioned Oats
¼ cup wheat germ
1 teaspoon baking soda
1 teaspoon cinnamon
¼ teaspoon nutmeg

Per serving:

85 calories
39% of calories from fat
1.3 gm protein
12.1 gm carbohydrates
1.1 tsp sugar
3.7 gm fat
27.1 mg sodium
0 mg cholesterol

In a small bowl combine the egg whites, vanilla extract, and raisins. Soak the raisins for 30 minutes.

In a large bowl beat the margarine and sugars until creamy. In a medium bowl combine the dry ingredients. Fold the dry ingredients into the creamed mixture and stir until well mixed. Stir in the egg whites and raisin mixture. Drop by teaspoonfuls onto ungreased cookie sheets. Bake at 375° for 8 to 9 minutes, or until lightly browned. Remove immediately from the cookie sheet onto waxed paper.

Variation: Instead of making cookies, you can make squares by pouring batter into a lightly sprayed 13 x 9-inch pan. Bake at 375° for 20 to 25 minutes.

Makes about 4 dozen cookies.

Snacktime can be healthy and pleasurable. Some suggestions are:

- *Graham crackers, popcorn, low-salt pretzels, fig bars, gingersnaps, and vanilla wafers are fine.*

- *Spread a bagel with jelly. Did you know that angel food cake does not have any cholesterol, and just a little fat? Serve it occasionally with fruit and top with nonfat yogurt.*

- *My children love cooked noodles or macaroni tossed with a little olive oil and Parmesan cheese. Or try the recipe for Yogurt Cheese Fruit Dip (page 32.)*

One-Bowl Peanut Butter Cookies

¾ cup honey
½ cup corn oil
¾ cup Skippy creamy peanut butter
1 egg
2 egg whites
½ tablespoon nonfat powdered milk
1 tablespoon low-sodium baking powder
1 teaspoon cinnamon
½ teaspoon mace
¼ teaspoon cloves
½ cup Quaker Old-Fashioned Oats
¾ cup raisins
1¼ cups whole-wheat flour

Per cookie:

77 calories
51% of calories from fat
2 gm protein
8.5 gm carbohydrates
0 tsp sugar
4.4 gm fat
27.4 mg sodium
5.7 mg cholesterol

In a small bowl soak the raisins in water for 30 minutes. Drain.

In a large bowl beat the honey and oil with an electric mixer for 4 to 5 minutes, until creamy. Add the peanut butter and blend. Beat in the eggs, milk, baking powder, and spices until blended. With a spoon mix in the raisins, oats, and flour. Drop by teaspoonfuls onto an ungreased cookie sheet. Bake at 325° for 10 minutes.

Makes 4 dozen cookies.

Kitchen patrol

Small children can wash fruits and vegetables, tear salad greens, and pour ingredients into a bowl and stir them.

Kids can help prepare cookie dough. They love to break the eggs, measure and pour liquids, stir the batter, and shape or spoon the dough onto cookie sheets.

Consider designating a "children's kitchen drawer" or shelf for their recipes, cookie cutters, aprons, oven mitts, measuring cups and spoons. Let your child decorate the recipe cards of successful dishes you have made together with drawings or magazine cutouts and keep them in a "kid's recipe box or file."

Raisin Cookies

A favorite treat at our house. These are packed with energy.

1 cup raisins
½ cup dried apricots
½ cup nonfat powdered milk
¾ teaspoon low-sodium baking powder
¼ teaspoon baking soda
¾ cup whole-wheat flour
⅛ cup wheat germ
½ cup Promise margarine
½ cup creamy peanut butter
1 cup brown sugar
2 egg whites
1 teaspoon vanilla extract
3 tablespoons skim milk
⅛ cup sunflower seeds
1 cup Quaker Old-Fashioned Oats

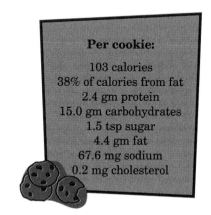

Per cookie:

103 calories
38% of calories from fat
2.4 gm protein
15.0 gm carbohydrates
1.5 tsp sugar
4.4 gm fat
67.6 mg sodium
0.2 mg cholesterol

Chop the raisins and apricots, and set aside.

In a medium bowl combine the powdered milk, baking powder, baking soda, flour, and wheat germ. Set aside.

In a large bowl cream the margarine and peanut butter. Add the brown sugar and beat until fluffy. Add the egg whites to the creamed mixture. Beat well. Stir in the vanilla and milk. Very slowly, stir in the flour mixture. Stir in the sunflower seeds and oats. The batter will be stiff. Add the raisins and apricots, stirring until well mixed. Drop by heaping tablespoonfuls onto an ungreased cookie sheet about 2½ inches apart. Bake at 350° for 10 to 15 minutes. Cool on waxed paper.

Makes 3 dozen cookies.

Honey Fruit Bars

A great Sunday school snack!

PAM baking spray
1½ cups peanut butter
1 cup honey
¾ cup brown sugar
5 cups raisin bran cereal
1 cup raisins

Spray a 13 x 9-inch pan with baking spray. In a medium saucepan combine the peanut butter, honey, and sugar. Bring the mixture to a boil over medium high heat, stirring constantly. Remove from the heat and stir in the remaining ingredients. Turn the mixture into the prepared pan. Using waxed paper, press the mixture down to distribute evenly in the pan. Cool for 15 minutes. Cut into 18 bars.

    Makes 18 bars.

Per bar:

176 calories
33% of calories from fat
4.7 gm protein
28.0 gm carbohydrates
1.8 tsp sugar
6.5 gm fat
150.0 mg sodium
0 mg cholesterol

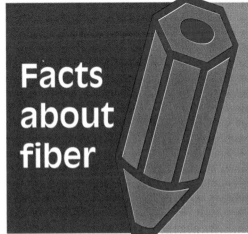

Facts about fiber

There are 2 kinds of fiber that we all need in our diets. Water-insoluble fiber is found in cereals and whole grains such as wheat bran. It increases stool bulk and makes it easier for waste to pass through the digestive tract.
    Water-soluble fiber is found in oats, oat bran, beans, legumes, corn, and some fruits and vegetables. It delays gastric emptying, slowing absorption of glucose from the small bowel. This helps lower serum cholesterol.

O'Brownies

PAM baking spray
2 egg whites, lightly beaten
⅔ cup sugar
⅛ cup water
2 tablespoons vegetable oil
½ teaspoon vanilla extract
½ cup all-purpose flour
⅛ cup Quaker Old-Fashioned Oats
¼ cup unsweetened cocoa
1½ teaspoons low-sodium baking powder
Powdered sugar (optional)

Per bar:

89 calories
25% of calories from fat
1.4 gm protein
15.7 gm carbohydrates
2.6 tsp sugar
2.5 gm fat
78.8 mg sodium
0 mg cholesterol

Spray an 8-inch square pan with baking spray. In a large bowl combine the egg whites, sugar, water, oil, and vanilla extract, stirring well.

In a separate bowl combine the dry ingredients. Add to the liquid mixture, stirring well. Pour the batter into the prepared pan. Bake at 350° for 20 to 25 minutes, or until a toothpick inserted in the middle comes out clean.

Makes 12 bars.

Plan for snack attacks

Make sure the refrigerator is stocked with nutritious snacks. Do not buy any other kind. Designate a shelf in the refrigerator and keep it stocked with fresh fruit.

Post a list on the refrigerator door with snack options and let your kids help themselves to any of those choices. Keep resealable plastic bags full of dried fruit, trail mix, grated low-fat cheese, whole-wheat crackers, pre-sliced lean meats, shredded carrots, and sliced fruits and vegetables in the refrigerator within easy reach.

Baked Apples

Serve warm with vanilla yogurt or splurge with vanilla ice cream.

4 Granny Smith apples
¼ cup chopped walnuts or pecans
2 tablespoons chopped dried dates
1 teaspoon cinnamon
2 tablespoons honey
2 teaspoons lemon juice
½ cup apple cider

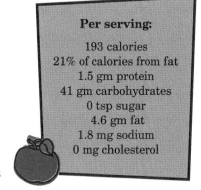

Per serving:

193 calories
21% of calories from fat
1.5 gm protein
41 gm carbohydrates
0 tsp sugar
4.6 gm fat
1.8 mg sodium
0 mg cholesterol

W ash the apples. Core out the center to 1 inch diameter, taking care not to core all the way through the bottom of apple. Set aside.

In a small bowl combine the nuts, dates, cinnamon, honey, and lemon juice. Mix well. Fill the apples with the nut mixture. Place the apples in a glass baking dish. Pour the apple cider into the dish. Bake at 375° for 45 minutes. Baste the apples with cider every 15 minutes.

Serves 4.

AaBbCcDdEeFfGgHhIiJjKkLlMmNnOoPpQqRrSsTtUuVvWwXxYyZz

Consider an apple a day to help fight the afternoon drowsy spell that many of us encounter. Apples contain the mineral boron, which affects general alertness and reaction times. A diet without boron can leave you sluggish.

Baked Pears

A pleasant warm dessert on a cold winter's eve. A dollop of vanilla nonfat yogurt makes a nice addition.

4 ripe Bosc pears
1½ tablespoons raisins
4 tablespoon orange juice
1 teaspoon brown sugar
½ teaspoon nutmeg
½ teaspoon cinnamon

Peel and core the pears. Stuff each pear with a teaspoon of raisins. Place in a glass baking dish. In a small bowl combine the remaining ingredients. Pour the mixture over the pears. Cover and microwave on high for 11 to 12 minutes, or until just tender when pricked with a fork.
    Serves 4.

Per serving:

121 calories
5% of calories from fat
0.8 gm protein
31.0 gm carbohydrates
0.3 tsp sugar
0.7 gm fat
0.8 mg sodium
0 mg cholesterol

Which food has the highest fat content: 1 cup of vanilla ice cream, 3 ounces of cooked beef sirloin steak, or 10 English walnuts?

The walnuts are highest, with 32 grams of fat. The ice cream has 14 grams of fat, and a steak trimmed of all fat has 8 grams of fat.

Which contains more saturated fat and cholesterol: 1 cup of vanilla ice cream, 3 ounces of cooked beef sirloin steak, or 10 English walnuts?

The ice cream has almost 9 grams of saturated fat and 59 milligrams of cholesterol per serving.

Brown Pineapple

1 16-ounce can unsweetened sliced pineapple, drained
1 tablespoon brown sugar
¼ teaspoon ground allspice

In a 9-inch square glass baking dish arrange the pineapple in a single layer. Sprinkle with the brown sugar and allspice. Cover with waxed paper and microwave on high for 5 minutes. Remove the waxed paper. Let the pineapple rest for 10 minutes before serving.

If you do not have a microwave, this recipe can also be baked in the oven. Bake uncovered at 350° for 10 minutes, or until the brown sugar melts and the pineapple is heated through.

Serves 4.

Per serving:

51 calories
7% of calories from fat
0.3 gm protein
13 gm carbohydrates
0.8 tsp sugar
0.4 gm fat
1.8 mg sodium
0 mg cholesterol

AaBbCcDdEeFfGgHhIiJjKkLlMmNnOoPpQqRrSsTtUuVvWwXxYyZz

Air-popped popcorn is a great snack with 90 calories and almost no fat in a 3-cup serving. Experiment with healthy seasonings such as butter substitute, garlic powder, chili powder, cayenne pepper, onion powder, Parmesan cheese, salt-free seasonings, or curry powder.

B. B. Freeze

Great on a hot summer evening.

1 large ripe banana
1 teaspoon lemon juice
½ cup strawberries
¼ cup frozen unsweetened apple juice concentrate

Slice the banana into a small bowl. Toss gently with the lemon juice so the banana slices are covered. In a small glass baking pan place the banana slices in a single layer. Cover with plastic wrap and freeze until firm.

In a blender combine the strawberries and banana slices and process until well chopped. Add the apple juice and process until smooth. Pour into small dessert bowls and serve right away.

Serves 4.

Per serving:

66 calories
4% of calories from fat
0.4 gm protein
14.4 gm carbohydrates
0.2 tsp sugar
0.3 gm fat
2.7 mg sodium
0 mg cholesterol

Children have small stomachs and cannot eat a lot of food at one time. Nutritious snacks can be used to fill the gap.

- *Peanut butter and low-fat, low-sodium crackers offer protein, complex carbohydrates, and monounsaturated fat.*

- *Whole-grain muffins and bagels offer fiber, complex carbohydrates, and B vitamins.*

- *Raw vegetables with nonfat yogurt dip offer complex carbohydrates, vitamin A, and some B vitamins.*

- *Unsalted pretzels and air-popped popcorn offer B vitamins.*

- *Rice cakes with fruit preserves offer complex carbohydrates.*

- *Frozen fruit yogurt or fruit juice pops offer vitamin C.*

- *Nuts or fruit mixed into nonfat yogurt offer vitamins A and D and calcium.*

- *Low-fat cheese offers calcium, protein, and needed fat.*

Orange Ice

A great treat on a hot summer day or when the flu season strikes and you are look-ing for an innovative way to introduce fluids and vitamin C.

2 cups water
1½ cups sugar
2 cups freshly squeezed orange juice (8 oranges)
½ cup lemon juice (1 lemon)

I n a medium saucepan bring the water and sugar to a boil. Continue boiling for 10 minutes over medium high heat. Remove from the heat and cool.

In a 2-quart casserole combine the orange juice and lemon juice. Stir in the sugar water. Cover with plastic wrap and place in the freezer. After 2 to 3 hours, just as the mixture begins to freeze, remove the mixture from the freezer and stir. Cover and return to the freezer for another 1 to 2 hours.

Scoop out and serve in small bowls.

Serves 8.

Per serving:
170 calories
0.5% of calories from fat
0.5 gm protein
43.5 gm carbohydrates
9 tsp sugar
0.1 gm fat
4.1 mg sodium
0 mg cholesterol

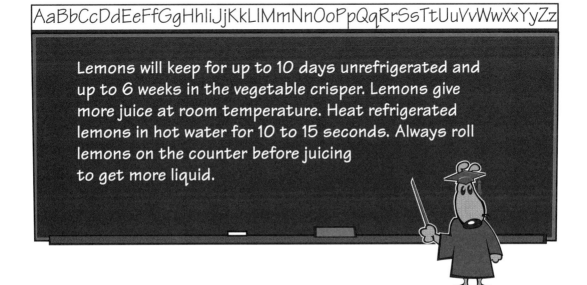

AaBbCcDdEeFfGgHhIiJjKkLlMmNnOoPpQqRrSsTtUuVvWwXxYyZz

Lemons will keep for up to 10 days unrefrigerated and up to 6 weeks in the vegetable crisper. Lemons give more juice at room temperature. Heat refrigerated lemons in hot water for 10 to 15 seconds. Always roll lemons on the counter before juicing to get more liquid.

Strawberry Sorbet

1 16-ounce package unsweetened frozen strawberries
3 tablespoons frozen unsweetened apple
  juice concentrate
⅔ cup plain nonfat yogurt
¼ cup nonfat powdered milk

Place ¼ of the strawberries in a blender. Chop, then purée. Add another ¼ of the strawberries and chop, then purée. Add the remaining strawberries and the apple juice concentrate, chop, and then purée. Add the yogurt and powdered milk and process until smooth. Pour into an 11 x 7-inch glass pan. Cover with plastic wrap and place in the freezer.

When almost frozen, return the mixture to the blender. Process until creamy. Spoon into 6 dessert dishes. Cover with plastic wrap and return to the freezer.

Remove from the freezer 15 minutes before serving.

Serves 6.

Per serving:

39 calories
0.7% of calories from fat
1.3 gm protein
8.5 gm carbohydrates
0 tsp sugar
0.3 gm fat
15.3 mg sodium
0.4 mg cholesterol

Uses for yogurt

Yogurt is a great product with many uses. It is a great source of calcium and protein. It has ¼ the calories of sour cream and up to ¼₄ the calories of mayonnaise. Use it as a substitute for both in dips, as a topping for fruits and desserts, in soups, salads, and elsewhere.

Yogurt does curdle at high temperatures. In cooking start with yogurt at room temperature. Always add the yogurt at the end of cooking and warm over low heat for a brief period.

Yogurt is great for breakfast, too. Top plain nonfat yogurt with wheat germ, bran, sliced bananas, fresh berries, granola, orange sections, or raisins.

Cranberry, Pineapple, and Yogurt Freeze

2 cups raw cranberries
¼ cup frozen unsweetened cherry juice concentrate
1 20-ounce can unsweetened crushed pineapple, drained
1 pint plain nonfat yogurt
3 ounces frozen unsweetened orange juice concentrate
½ cup Grape-Nuts

Per serving:

46 calories
0.4% of calories from fat
1.3 gm protein
10.3 mg carbohydrates
0.1 tsp sugar
0.2 mg fat
23.9 mg sodium
0.4 mg cholesterol

In a blender chop the cranberries. Add the cherry juice and marinate for 30 minutes.

Add the remaining ingredients except the Grape-Nuts, and blend.

Line 12 muffin cups with foil muffin liners. Fill each with cranberry mixture and top with the Grape-Nuts. Freeze for 6 hours, or until firm. Remove from the freezer 15 minutes before serving.

Serves 12.

AaBbCcDdEeFfGgHhIiJjKkLlMmNnOoPpQqRrSsTtUuVvWwXxYyZz

For a festive, grown-up dessert, serve chunks of watermelon, strawberries, blueberries, fresh peaches, or any summer fruits in plastic wine glasses and top with nonfat yogurt or lemon and mint.

Energy Snacks

My children love to have their portion in resealable bags for a snack in the car.

3 tablespoons raisins
4 tablespoons raw unsalted shelled peanuts
4 tablespoons unsalted shelled sunflower seeds
3 tablespoons coconut
3 tablespoons chocolate chips

Mix together all of the ingredients. Store in an airtight plastic container.
Serves 4.

Per serving:

229 calories
64% of calories from fat
6.7 gm protein
18.6 gm carbohydrates
1.0 tsp sugar
16.4 gm fat
5.9 mg sodium
0 mg cholesterol

Pumpkin Seeds

PAM baking spray
1 cup pumpkin seeds
Salt substitute seasoning

Spray a glass dish with baking spray.
Rinse the seeds in water to remover the fibers. Pat dry with a paper towel. Place the seeds in the prepared dish. Sprinkle lightly with nonsalt seasoning.
    Microwave on high for 5 to 6 minutes or until the seeds are crisp, stirring after every minute. Let the seeds rest for 5 minutes.
    Serves 4.

Per serving:

194 calories
76% of calories from fat
10.2 gm protein
5.3 gm carbohydrates
0 tsp sugar
16.4 gm fat
0 mg sodium
0 mg cholesterol

Craft
Recipes

Birdfeeder

String
Creamy peanut butter
Medium size, (3-inch) pine cones
1 cup any type birdseed

Attach the string by tying a knot to the pine cone stem. With a knife, spread the peanut butter all over the pine cone. Place the birdseed in a pie tin. Roll the pine cones in the birdseed until covered. Hang the pine cones high on a tree out of reach of any cats. The birds will be grateful!

Clay

2 cups baking soda
1¼ cups cold water
1 cup cornstarch

In a medium saucepan combine all of the ingredients. Over medium heat cook the mixture for 4 to 5 minutes, or until it thickens and pulls away from the sides of the pan. With a spoon transfer the clay to a pie tin. Cover with a damp cloth and allow to cool.

On a flat surface covered with waxed paper knead the clay for 2 minutes.

Sculpt as desired, then allow to dry overnight on a piece of waxed paper. Paint with acrylic colors and shellac.

Store any remaining clay in a resealable bag.

Finger Paints

3 tablespoons sugar
½ cup cornstarch
2 cups cold water
Ivory liquid soap
Food coloring of choice

In a medium saucepan over medium low heat combine the sugar and cornstarch. Stir well and add the cold water. Stir constantly until well blended and the mixture begins to thicken, about 15 minutes.

Divide the mixture into 4 or 5 plastic containers such as margarine tubs. Add food coloring to make the desired colors and add a couple of drops of Ivory liquid soap to help with the cleanup.

Be sure to spread newspaper over the "artist's" work area and dress appropriately for messy fun. Create masterpieces on fingerpaint paper, butcher paper, or even waxed paper.

Playdough

1 cup all-purpose flour
1 cup water
½ cup salt
1 tablespoon corn oil
2 tablespoons cream of tartar
Food color of choice

In a large saucepan combine all of the ingredients. Cook over medium high heat, stirring constantly until the dough pulls away from the sides of the pan. Cool, then knead.

Lots of fun, inexpensive, and nontoxic! You can divide the recipe in half and use two different colors.

Silly Puddy

2 parts white Elmer's glue (not school glue)
1 part Stayflo liquid starch

Combine the ingredients in a small bowl. Try ¼ cup of glue and ⅛ cup of starch. Allow the puddy to dry for 30 minutes to 1 hour before it will be workable. Store the puddy in an airtight container. This recipe may not work on a humid day.

Keep the puddy away from clothes, carpet, etc. This is toxic and should not be eaten or given to small children.

Silly puddy will bounce and pick up newsprint.

Crystal Gardens

4 tablespoons salt
4 tablespoons water
1 tablespoon ammonia
2 pieces charcoal, broken into small pieces with a hammer
Pie tin
Food coloring

In a small bowl combine the salt, water, and ammonia. Place the charcoal in the bottom of the pan. Place drops of different food coloring in various locations. Set the pan in an easy location (such as the kitchen counter) and watch the colorful crystal garden grow!

Paint with Soap Bubbles

Ivory Flakes
Water
Food coloring
Waxed paper

Boxed ready-made flakes are hard to get now. If necessary, shave bars of Ivory soap into flakes with a kitchen knife or cheese grater.

In a large bowl combine the shavings of 1 bar of soap with ¼ cup of warm water. The mixture should be thick and creamy. Add food coloring and whip with an electric mixer until fluffy. Repeat in separate bowls for other colors as desired.

Finger paint on waxed paper or make sculptures. Remind your children not to rub their eyes or face with their hands until they have been thoroughly washed!

Soap Carving

This project should be supervised by an adult. It is for children 5 years and older with good motor control and eye-hand coordination.

Ivory soap bars
Dull kitchen knife
Pencil or toothpick

Have the child draw an outline of the desired scupture on the soap with a pencil or toothpick. Use a dull kitchen knife to carve out the shape. Hearts, bells, Christmas trees, and other simple shapes work best.

When finished, use the soap for the child's bath, or shave it to make Paint with Soap Bubbles.

Environmental Health

Counter Cleaner

Spray bottle
Water
White vinegar
Salt

In a spray bottle combine water and vinegar in 1 to 1 proportion. To every quart, add 1 teaspoon of salt.

Use this mixture to clean kitchen and bathroom counters, as well as the kitchen table and plastic placemats.

Floor Cleaner

White vinegar
Hot water

Sweep and dust the floors to be cleaned. In a pail combine vinegar and water in 1 to 4 proportion. Mop the floors with the mixture. This is usually recommended for wood floors.

Sink Cleaner

¼ cup borax
½ lemon

Rinse the stainless steel sink with water. Sprinkle borax around sink. Use the lemon like a sponge to scrub the sink clean.

A lemon slice is a great garbage disposal freshener.

Toilet Bowl Cleaner

Baking soda
Scrub brush

Sprinkle 1 cup of baking soda around the inside of the toilet bowl. Let it soak for 5 minutes. Scrub with a toilet brush. Flush.

If every household used natural cleaners, it would prevent 32 million pounds of chemical waste each day from entering the water supply.

Recycle

Don't forget to recycle your glass, plastic, aluminum, and newspapers! We have four boxes set up in the garage for this purpose.

If your state does not have mandatory recycling, check with your local grocery store or in the yellow pages for a recycling outlet.

Buy groceries in large containers rather than individual-sized packages. This cuts down on waste and saves money, too.

Use waxed paper for many of the things you use plastic wrap for, such as microwaving or wrapping items for the refrigerator. It is ecologically better and costs a lot less. Wash and reuse plastic wrap and resealable bags, as well as aluminum foil.

Use pump bottles that are refillable rather than aerosols, and whenever possible make your own cleaners.

Buy food in recyclable containers. Those plastic shakers of pancake mix cost a lot more and aren't recyclable, nor are the squeeze bottles for ketchup, jams, and salad dressings. Some plastic containers claim to be recyclable but are not accepted yet by most recycling centers. Buy frozen foods packaged in cardboard rather than plastic or styrofoam. They're ecologically better, and less expensive.

Household Ideas

Replace light bulbs as they burn out with compact fluorescent bulbs. They last a lot longer and save a lot of energy.

Replace or clean furnace air filters and air conditioner filters at least 4 times a year. This will make the furnace or air conditioner more efficient, not to mention keeping the air fresher.

Turn on the "power saver" switch in your refrigerator if it has one.

Change your shower head to a water-saving low-flow shower head. They are inexpensive and will save on your total energy bill.

If every household in the United States turned down the thermostat by 3 degrees, we'd save 250,000 barrels of oil a day. Reduce the temperature on the water heater by 10 degrees and save 3 to 5 percent on the heating bill.

Reduce the amount of paper you send to the landfill by eliminating your name from junk mailing lists. Write to Mail Preference Service Direct Marketing Association, 11 West 42nd Street, P.O. Box 3861, New York, New York, 10163-3861. This will stop your name from being sold to many mailing list companies.

Environmental Facts

If every household recycled newspapers and aluminum cans, this would save 1 million trees every 2 weeks and save enough metal to rebuild our entire commercial air fleet every 3 months.

Each year we dump between 10 and 20 times the amount of oil spilled by the *Exxon Valdez.* If we all kept our tires properly inflated, America would save $2 million, 300,000 tons of pollution, and 3 supertankers of oil a day. If everyone kept their automobiles tuned, this would save an additional $45 million and 13,000 tons of pollution.

A glass bottle sent to the landfill this year could still be around in 2993.

Americans throw away 1.6 billion disposable pens and 2.2 billion disposable razors each year.

Americans make up 5 percent of the world's population, but use 25 percent of its resources and 30 percent of its energy.

One of every $11 we spend at the grocery pays for packaging. If we reduced the amount of packaging we brought home by one-half, the trash going to landfills would be cut by 15 percent and paper use would be cut by 25 percent.

Menu Ideas

Week One

Sunday	Pasta Primavera, page 81; Grapefruit
Monday	Limey Chicken, page 92; Couscous
Tuesday	Minestrone, page 20; Green Salad, page 29; Sourdough Rolls
Wednesday	Grilled Halibut, page 105; Yellow Rice, page 132; Steamed Brussels Sprouts, page 120
Thursday	Polish Kielbasa Casserole, page 109; Fruit Soup, page 18
Friday	Veggie Sandwich, page 72; Hearty Mushroom Soup, page 22
Saturday	Tuna Pasta Salad, page 44; Sweet Yellow Slaw, page 34

Week Two

Sunday	Marinated Fish Steaks, page 105; Parslied Boiled and Baked Potatoes, page 125; Green Flowers, page 122
Monday	Easy Bean Burritos, page 113; Tomato Rice, page 129; Grapefruit
Tuesday	White (Cauliflower) Soup, page 24; Cinnamon Muffins, page 51; Peach Slices
Wednesday	Chicken and Bulgur, page 87; Easter Bunny Salad, page 35
Thursday	Vegetarian Stir-Fry, page 118; White or Brown Rice; Rise and Shine, page 37
Friday	Ground Beef and Linguine, page 74; Green Salad, page 29
Saturday	Cream Cheese and Cucumber Sandwich, page 70; Ants on a Log, page 122; Salsa Dip with Blue Corn Tortilla Chips, page 64

Week Three

Sunday	Pork Chops, page 110; Orzo; Popeye's Spinach Salad, page 32
Monday	Veggie Burritos with Guacamole Topping, page 116; Shredded Lettuce and Diced Tomatoes
Tuesday	Fancy Steamed Salmon, page 102; Baked New Potatoes; Sweet Carrots, page 123
Wednesday	The Bullfighter's Rice, page 112; Orange Slices
Thursday	Vegetable-Rice Soup, page 23; Nutty Raisin Muffins, page 54
Friday	Chicken with Orange Sauce, page 88; Pasta and Vegetable Salad, page 30; Fruit Delight, page 35
Saturday	Spaghetti with Raisins, page 82; Sourdough Bread Lettuce and Tomato Salad

Week Four

Sunday	Turkey Chili, page 98; Corn Bread, page 59; Rise and Shine, page 37
Monday	Lemon Chicken, page 91; Plain Potatoes, page 126 Baked Tomatoes, page 128
Tuesday	Carrot and Tomato Soup, page 15; Spinach Salad with Poppy Seed Dressing, page 33; Apple Muffins, page 48
Wednesday	Beef and Barley, page 106; Applesauce
Thursday	Tostadas, page 97; Cantaloupe
Friday	Tuna Rice Salad, page 45; Sweet Blueberry Muffins, page 50
Saturday	Mama's Spaghetti Sauce, page 78; Creamy Cucumber Salad, page 29

Week Five

Sunday	Pappy's Pasta, page 80; Thin Spaghetti Strawberry Sorbet, page 148
Monday	Fish Creole, page 103; Green Salad, page 29 Brown Pineapple, page 145
Tuesday	Mexican Taco Salad, page 46; Chilled Pears and Low-Fat Cottage Cheese
Wednesday	East Indian Chicken Soup, page 17; Chilled Apricots
Thursday	Broccoli and Tofu, page 121; Red Apple Slice Yogurt Cheese Fruit Dip, page 32
Friday	Vegetarian Lasagna, page 84; Hawaiian Fruit Salad, page 36 French Bread
Saturday	Rice and Broccoli Bake, page 111; Fresh Fruit Salad, page 36

Week Six

Sunday	Marinated Fish Steaks, page 105; Italian Beans, page 120 Potato Salad, page 31
Monday	Turkey Chef's Salad, page 43; Banana Bread, page 57
Tuesday	Beet Red Soup, page 14; Mushroom Potato Pie, page 124
Wednesday	Paella, page 93; Orange Slices
Thursday	Meatballs in Tomato Sauce, page 79; Baked Pears, page 144 Grapes
Friday	Chicken Salad with Couscous, page 42; Pumpkin Muffins, page 55
Saturday	Grilled Chicken; Corn Salad, page 28; Mashed Potatoes

Bibliography

Books

Barone, Jeanine, M.S.; Carter, Betty Jean, M.S.; Cohn, Lisa, MMSc, R.D.; Cross, Donna, GDHS; Spark, Arlene, EdD, R.D.; Williams, Christine L., M.D.; and Wynder, Ernst L., M.D. *Great Meals Great Snacks*. New York: American Foundation, 1989.

Brody, Jane. *Jane Brody's Good Food Book*. New York: Bantam Books, 1987.

Epstein, Leonard H., Ph.D., and Squires, Sally, M.S. *The Stop-Light Diet for Children*. Boston: Little, Brown, and Company, 1988.

Lambert-Lagace, Louise. *Feeding Your Children from Infancy to Six Years Old*. Ontario: General Publishing Co., Ltd., 1982.

Lansky, Vicki. *Feed Me I'm Yours*. Wayzata, Minn.: Meadowbrook Press, 1974.

———. *The Taming of the C.A.N.D.Y. Monster*. Deephaven, Minn.: Meadowbrook Press, 1987.

Lappe, Frances Moore. *Diet for a Small Planet*. New York: Ballantine Books, 1971.

Moore, Kathi. *Good Food Good Kids, Provided for You by Rose Women's Center and None Such, Ltd.* Denver.

Morgan, Brian L. G. *The Lifelong Nutrition Guide, How to Eat for Health at Every Age and Stage of Life*. Englewood Cliffs, NJ: Prentice Hall, 1983.

Roth, Harriet. *Deliciously Low*. New York: New American Library, 1984.

Whelan, Elizabeth M., M.D., and Stare, Frederick J., M.D. *The 100% Natural, Purely Organic, Cholesterol-Free, Megavitamin, Low-Carbohydrate Nutrition Hoax*. New York: Atheneum, 1983.

Winnick, Muron, M.D. *Growing Up Healthy*. New York: William Morrow and Company, Inc. 1982.

Magazine Articles

Breir, Leah C. "Dr. Michael Debakey on How to Take Care of Your Heart." *Family Circle,* October 1987, pp. 38, 57.

Challem, Jack Joseph, and Lewin, Renate. "Cholesterol and Heart Disease: The Debate Continues." *Let's Live,* March 1989, pp. 55-59.

Gannes, Stuart. "Behind the Batle over Cholesterol." *Fortune,* December 18, 1989, pp. 101, 104-105, 110, 116.

Ulene, Art, M.D. "A 30-Day Plan to Lower Your Cholesterol." *Good Housekeeping,* March 1989, pp. 77,80, 82, 84-88.

"The ABC's of Omega 3's." *Weight Watchers' Magazine,* Feburary 1989, p. 20.

"Cabbage." *Good Housekeeping,* March 1989, p.168.

"Food and Health: Power Breakfast in a Bowl: A Quick Guide to Cold Cereals."

"Food for Thought: The Dish on Fish." *Self,* January 1989, p.146.

"The Liquid-Diet Craze, Why Doctors Say 'Watch Out'." *Good Housekeeping,* March 1989, pp. 205-206.

"Number's Game." *Weight Watchers' Magazine,* Febuary 1989, pp. 13, 16-17.

"We Mean Lean." *Weight Watchers' Magazine,* February 1989, p. 10.

Newspaper Articles

Parade Magazine, March 19, 1989

Parade Magazine, August 20, 1989

Rocky Mountain News, "Nutriition and You." October 29, 1989

Rocky Mountain News, August 31, 1989

Rocky Mountain News, June 13, 1989

Rocky Mountain News, Febuary 28, 1989

Rocky Mountain News, "Fiber." Febuary 22, 1989

Rocky Mountain News, "Hostility Tied to Heart Desease." January 17, 1989

Rocky Mountain News, "The Oat Bran Myth? Study Questions Touted Benefits." January 18, 1990

Rocky Mountain News, Lifestyles, May 10, 1989

Rocky Mountain News, March 25, 1990

Pamphlets

Cooking Maverick Ranch Lite Beef. Maverick Ranch Lite Beef. 1989.

Diet, Nutrition, and Cancer Prevention. United States Dept. of Health and Human Services and NCI.

Eating for Life. National Institute of Health. June 1988.

Eating Well Can Help Your Child Learn Better. International Reading Association.

Kiddie Letter. Cooperative Extension, Colorado State University. January, February, 1989.

National Cholesterol Education Program: *Report of the Expert Panel on Blood Cholesterol Levels in Children and Adolescents,* U.S. Department of Health and Human Services, Public Health Services, National Institutes of Health, September 1991

Computer Software Programs

Guttmann, Naomi D., M.S., L.D., and Uhrich, Roberta V. M.S., L.S., *Nutritional Data Resources: Dietwise.* Willoughby, Ohio, 1984.

Index

A

T

V

Ann Schrader is president of Yellowstone Promotions, Inc., an advertising specialty business. A graduate of the University of Northern Colorado, she lives in Englewood, Colorado, with her husband and two children. Good nutrition and healthy family cooking have been longtime pursuits.